M. Jeff Thompson

~

T0163339

PROJECT SPONSORS

Missouri Center for the Book

Western Historical Manuscript Collection,
University of Missouri–Columbia

SPECIAL THANKS

Robert L. Dyer, Songteller, Boonville, Missouri
Christine Montgomery, State Historical Society of Missouri, Columbia
Claudia Powell, Western Historical Manuscript Collection,
University of Missouri–Columbia

MISSOURI HERITAGE READERS
General Editor, Rebecca B. Schroeder

Each Missouri Heritage Reader explores a particular aspect of the state's rich cultural heritage. Focusing on people, places, historical events, and the details of daily life, these books illustrate the ways in which people from all parts of the world contributed to the development of the state and the region. The books incorporate documentary and oral history, folklore, and informal literature in a way that makes these resources accessible to all Missourians.

Intended primarily for adult new readers, these books will also be invaluable to readers of all ages interested in the cultural and social history of Missouri.

OTHER BOOKS IN THE SERIES

M. Jeff Thompson

Missouri's Swamp Fox of the Confederacy

Doris Land Mueller

University of Missouri Press
Columbia and London

Copyright © 2007 by
The Curators of the University of Missouri
University of Missouri Press, Columbia, Missouri 65201
Printed and bound in the United States of America
All rights reserved
5 4 3 2 1   11 10 09 08 07

Library of Congress Cataloging-in-Publication Data

Mueller, Doris Land, 1927-
M. Jeff Thompson : Missouri's swamp fox of the Confederacy / Doris Land
Mueller.
p. cm. — (Missouri heritage readers)
Summary: "Doris Land Mueller offers an adventurous account of the life of
Confederate Army commander Meriwether Jeff Thompson. Thompson's mili-
tary exploits in the Missouri Bootheel region earned him the nicknamed
"Swamp Fox" from Union General Ulysses S. Grant, while his writing earned
him the nickname "Poet Laureate of the Marshes"—Provided by publisher.
Includes bibliographical references and index.
ISBN 978-0-8262-1724-0 (pbk. : alk. paper)
1. Thompson, Meriwether Jeff, 1826-1876. 2. Generals—Confederate States
of America—Biography. 3. Confederate States of America. Army—Biography.
4. Missouri—History—Civil War, 1861-1865—Campaigns. 5. United States—
History—Civil War, 1861-1865—Campaigns. 6. Missouri—Biography. I. Title.
E467.1.T47M84 2007
973.7'3092—dc22
[B]
2006102250

♾️™ This paper meets the requirements of the
American National Standard for Permanence of Paper
for Printed Library Materials, Z39.48, 1984.

Designer: Douglas Freeman
Typesetter: FoleyDesign
Printer and binder: Thomson-Shore, Inc.
Typefaces: Palatino and Old Claude

To my husband, Jack—

My first reader, most steadfast supporter, and dearest friend

Contents

~

Acknowledgments

~

J ust as it "takes a village" to rear a child, so does it take a host of helpmeets to create a book. Even before I had written the first word, John C. Fisher, author of *Catfish, Fiddles, Mules, and More: Missouri's State Symbols*, encouraged me and helped me to believe I could successfully complete the project. The patient librarians of the St. Louis, St. Louis County, Jefferson County, and St. Joseph, Missouri, libraries were most generous in their efforts to locate sources and obtain copies of various materials. The staff of the Missouri Historical Society and the State Historical Society of Missouri in Columbia, the Ohio Historical Society, and the University of North Carolina at Chapel Hill cooperated fully in providing print and microfilm materials. Leon Cahill Miller, Manuscripts Librarian for the Howard-Tilden Memorial Library Special Collections at Tulane University, was especially helpful in making available a broad range of letters, poems, and other Thompson-related documents for my study.

I am also deeply grateful to Jody Feldman, Maggie Fowler, and Kate Raybuck, veteran members of our small critique group, who read, reread, and offered suggestions on every draft of every chapter.

Most of all, I want to express my appreciation to Editor Rebecca B. Schroeder for her unswerving support and gentle guidance throughout the course of the book's preparation. Becky is the editor every author longs to have. She has given unstintingly of her time and energy in an effort to make this book as good as possible.

M. Jeff Thompson

The Swamp Fox

Brave sons of Missouri, come turn out. If your hearts are
 with us, give a shout
Leave your yokes and leave your plows. The cattle on a
 thousand hills are ours.
Come join the Swamp Fox Thompson's men. Heel of the
 boot is the Fox's den,
He knows the land of the sweet gum tree, like a salt sea
 sailor knows the sea.

Chorus: Down in the swamp east, low lands low
          Come follow wherever Jeff Thompson goes,
          Hold on boys, don't lose your grip
          When I give the word boys, let it rip!

He rides by day and strikes by night. He's a real rip-
 squealer and his name is Fight.
He strikes like the winds of the hurricane to drive the
 invaders out of our land.
We crossed over Mingo Swamp one night with a thousand
 torches for our light.
That's a story that years from now will still be told by the
 minks and the owls.

— Bob Dyer, from *Rebel in the Woods: Civil War Songs from the
 Western Border, Vol. II,* Cathy Barton, Dave Para, Bob Dyer

1

Swamp Fox

A Badge of Honor in American History

~

Why might someone be called a "swamp fox"? Imagine being in a swamp at dawn, a place filled with strange smells, mysterious sounds, and treacherous pockets of quicksand. Suddenly a fox appears, trotting confidently along seeking food for himself and his family. He moves quickly and silently, almost invisibly, easily avoiding traps or other dangers, until he finds and seizes an unwary frog or bird and carries it triumphantly back to his den. Once again he has lived up to his reputation for cunning and cleverness.

A person who, like the fox, can successfully navigate swamplands, often at night, adeptly evading enemies who seek to capture him and then striking them unexpectedly, may be compared to a swamp fox. M. Jeff Thompson was such a person.

Although he holds the title of Missouri's "Swamp Fox," Thompson was not the first military leader in American history to be given that name. That honor goes to Francis Marion, a colonial soldier during the Revolutionary War. Not a great deal is known about Marion's early life. He was born near Georgetown, South Carolina, probably in 1732, the youngest of six children. He was unusually small at birth, with underdeveloped legs and ankles that troubled him all his life. No one would call him handsome—he had a large head, a long nose, and a small body.

Born in Harpers Ferry, Virginia, in 1826, M. Jeff Thompson settled in western Missouri in 1847 and soon became active in the state militia. Historians believe this photograph shows him as a colonel and division inspector in the prewar Missouri Volunteer Militia in about 1860. *State Historical Society of Missouri, Columbia.*

As he grew up, he was sickly and didn't have many friends or playmates. His main companion was Oscar, his personal, or "body," servant, who was raised with Francis. The two remained close friends throughout life.

From the time he was a young man, Francis Marion loved the swamps. He enjoyed hunting for wild game or roaming in the swampy low country from Charleston to Georgetown. Often he would stay out in the swamps for days at a time. He always carried a sword and pistols even though his sword was rusty and he was a poor shot with his pistols. He valued horses and always took good care of his own. Because of his weak legs, being able to ride was essential to his becoming a successful soldier.

Marion got his first military experience fighting the Cherokee Indians during the French and Indian War. Although the French had wanted them to continue fighting the British, the Cherokees asked for peace in September 1760. The British refused, and General Jeffrey Amherst ordered Colonel James Grant to Charleston to invade the Cherokee country. The Cherokees ambushed Grant and Francis Marion's Carolina Rangers at Etchoe Pass in June 1761. That experience taught Marion to avoid open combat and use ambush and surprise when fighting against greater numbers. He learned to strike his enemies in the early morning when they would be least prepared. These valuable tactics helped prepare him for guerrilla-style fighting against the British later in his career.

In 1775 the first provincial congress of South Carolina commissioned Marion as captain of the Second South Carolina Regiment. In that same year he was promoted to major, and in 1776 to lieutenant colonel. Four years later he was appointed brigadier general of the South Carolina militia. Marion performed brilliantly as a commander of these volunteer troops. With his small band of loyal colonials, he harassed the British forces unmercifully. Moving south, the British had expected to find many in the Carolinas loyal to the king. Instead they found bands of Patriots who were ready to fight. Historian Lucien Agniel wrote that the darkest moments of the war occurred following the defeat of General Horatio Gates at Camden, South Carolina, in August 1780 by Lord Charles Cornwallis, British commander of the southern campaigns of the Revolutionary War. With Gates's troops scattered, "the outcome of the war . . . lay in the hearts and hands of the fabled Southern guerrillas." He described Marion as "Preeminent among the Patriot

Guerrillas, a seasoned veteran of 48," whose band included former slaves as well as white Patriots. Providing intelligence to General Nathaniel Greene, his scouts tracked the movements of the British, and, when least expected, his men struck blow after blow against Cornwallis. Marion and his men became the terror of the British troops. Using hit-and-run tactics, Marion would attack, then retreat to the Carolina swamps well beyond the reach of his pursuers. In 1780 a British colonel, in utter frustration, called him a "damned old fox," and another Briton added that the devil himself could not catch him. This was when they began calling Francis Marion the Swamp Fox. After his defeat in South Carolina, Cornwallis wrote on January 21, 1781, "The late affair has almost broke my heart." He was to surrender at Yorktown, Virginia, before the end of the year.

When the war was over, General Marion summoned his brigade together one last time to express to them his thanks for their patience and fortitude. He assured them that "no citizens in the world could have done more" than they had done. Then the Swamp Fox and his friend Oscar got on their horses and rode off, back to civilian life. Marion died in 1795, but his legend has lived on in song and story.

In a stanza from "Song of Marion's Men," poet William Cullen Bryant wrote of the night rides of the Swamp Fox of the Revolutionary War that inspired Jeff Thompson's men in 1861:

> Well knows the fair and friendly moon
> The band that Marion leads
> The glittering of their rifles
> The scampering of their steeds.

Early in the Civil War, Confederate leader M. Jeff Thompson received the nickname "Swamp Fox" from Union General Ulysses S. Grant and others. He earned the title by rapidly marching and countermarching his men through the swamps of southeast Missouri, popping up unexpectedly in various places to confuse and frustrate the enemy. He realized that although the Federal troops were too strong for his small force, he could harass and worry them, and this he did. He devised ways to move his men quickly whenever necessary to meet the military need, while leading the Union authorities to believe he had more men than he actually did. For example, he would send squads with horses to a designated spot, and other squads to a different location where swamp boats or canoes waited. Then he would hit the enemy at one place, hurry to the next rendezvous point, and use boats to cross a swamp to where horses were waiting. By carrying out several small actions in various places using the same men, he was able to give the impression of a larger force and thus tie up more Federal troops.

In his book *Westerners in Gray: The Men and Missions of the Elite Fifth Missouri Infantry Regiment,* Phillip Tucker writes that Thompson and his men, who became known as the Swamp Fox Brigade, adopted the motto "Remember Marion . . . and dye every path, river, and bayou with the blood of the ruthless invaders." Their memories of the success stories of colonial bands in the American Revolution served to rekindle a guerrilla tradition that helped to give these Missouri rebels their nickname of swamp foxes. They burned bridges, tore up railroad tracks, ambushed Union patrols, and cut down telegraph wires.

When Thompson and his men were on the move, they traveled fast and light, and always carried salt in their pockets because they lived almost entirely on beef from cattle they foraged. As Thompson explained it in his memoirs:

> We would stop at a cornfield to feed our horses. There were beeves around every field, then one would be selected, shot down, skinned, cut up, issued to the men, cooked on coals, and eaten before the horses were done with their food . . . . Fastidious people at home can hardly believe that I have eaten beef that thirty minutes before was on its feet.

Jeff Thompson was at least as big a nuisance to the Union forces during the Civil War as his predecessor Francis Marion had been to the British in the Revolutionary War. His activities were one of the reasons that General John Charles Fremont, newly appointed Commander of the West in St. Louis, ordered General Grant from Jefferson City to Cape Girardeau only a week after Grant's arrival in the state capital on August 21, 1861. But again and again the Swamp Fox easily avoided being caught. On January 24, 1862, one newspaper, the *Missouri Statesman* in Columbia, proclaimed Thompson to be the "Marion of this revolution." Another newspaper described him as "the Marion of the South." Although not actually a guerrilla group, Thompson and his men were well acquainted with guerrilla tactics, and because of their elusiveness and hit-and-run tactics, his men were sometimes called Swamp Rats or Muskrats. An article in the *Statesman* even referred to Thompson as the "Hibernian Flea" because he seemed to be here, there, and everywhere, all at once. On still another occasion, the same newspaper dubbed him "Swamp Shark."

Carolyn Bartels's book *The Civil War in Missouri Day by Day 1861-1865* is peppered with references to Thompson, whom she calls the "wily Swamp Fox." For example, she writes that on October 15, 1861, at the Big River Bridge, "Thompson succeeded in capturing some 66 much needed guns and some not so needed prisoners." On October 18, 1861, "he was successful today in driving back Colonel Carlin's forces toward Pilot Knob." And, on December 29, 1861, he was "readying for descent upon Commerce to join others of his force."

Jeff Thompson greatly enjoyed the press coverage of his exploits as he and his troops slogged through the swamps of Missouri's Bootheel country, an area that had been devastated by the New Madrid earthquakes of 1811–1812. He was adept at manipulating the press to boost Southern morale and confuse the enemy. His favorite hiding ground was the Great Mingo Swamp, an area five to twenty-five miles wide that stretched north from the Arkansas-Missouri border to an area parallel to Cape Girardeau, Missouri. The old road leading through this swamp had not been repaired in years and in places was nearly unusable—except for Thompson's band. No better terrain could have been constructed for him and his men, who excelled at horsemanship, swimming, canoe paddling, and moving easily through a wilderness.

After one successful encounter with enemy troops in which a Union officer, Captain Isaac H. Elliott, had been shot in the arm, Thompson dressed the man's wound himself. When the officer couldn't believe he had been taken prisoner by the famous Swamp Fox, Thompson dramatically dipped his pen in some spilled ink, gave the officer his autograph, and told him to go back to Illinois and leave the Confederacy alone.

Thompson was like a phantom. By moving rapidly and issuing misleading proclamations and other communications, he kept the enemy in the dark as to his real strength. On most of his raids, his actual numbers were five hundred or fewer. Newspapers helped his cause by carrying frequent reports of the Swamp Fox having evaded traps set for him in the swamps of "boot country." Robert Hereford, in his book *Old Man River: The Memories of Captain Louis Rosche,* tells that when Rosche as a boy asked a Union soldier who the Swamp Fox was, the answer was:

> I ain't never seen him, but I've heard the whine of his bullets many a time. The Swamp Fox is a consarned, cocky, little feller that turns out one of the biggest fightin' jobs there is in this war. He's a ghost, the Swamp Fox is. Cain't never tell whether the varmint has six or sixty thousand men. You never get close enough to see him. He seems always to be doin' the runnin', but the other fellow's the one that's gettin' shot.

Because Jeff Thompson was so successful at using the tactics of psychological warfare, he was a constant thorn in the side of the Union forces. A typical frustrated commentary attesting to that fact appeared in a St. Louis newspaper, the *Missouri Republican,* on November 23, 1861:

We cannot fight him on his own ground . . . he has with him a crowd of Missouri swampers, who know every inch of the woods, lakes, and creeks in that region; he is incumbered by no baggage trains and but little artillery and he can move with the utmost celerity, defying any efforts of our men to find him, or follow if they can find him.

2

Thompson's Early Years

Meriwether Thompson, the fourth of six children, was born on January 22, 1826, in the historic community of Harpers Ferry, Virginia (now West Virginia). A number of his ancestors had served as officers in the Revolutionary War, and through his mother, Martha Slaughter Broadus, young Thompson was related to George Washington. His father, Captain Meriwether Thompson, served in the paymaster's department of the U.S. Army. With this background, it is not surprising that Meriwether and his family expected that he too would follow a military career.

But unlike his scholarly oldest brother, Broadus, who appreciated Shakespeare and Byron and always conformed to social standards, young Meriwether was not simply a follower of tradition; he was by nature more independent. He would rather explore the Harpers Ferry arsenal than go to school. He was fascinated by the arsenal with its stores of war machinery and equipment. As a young boy his favorite toys were cast-off weapons, and he showed an early interest and skill in taking muskets and pistols apart and putting them together again. His own comment on his childhood, in one of his typically short, concise diary entries, was, "No incidents worth relating except my knowledge of machinery, especially the locomotive engine, after the Baltimore and Ohio Railroad and Winchester and Potomac Railroads were built to Harpers Ferry."

Trapper and trader Joseph Robidoux III, founder of St. Joseph, settled at the Black Snake Hills post in the 1830s and was instrumental in helping to negotiate a peaceful settlement of the Platte Purchase. *Photograph by A. E. Schroeder of portrait in the St. Joseph Public Library, 1980.*

He often played hooky from school, preferring instead to ride around in a rickety old cart with an elderly black deliveryman named Jeff Carlyle. Meriwether's family disapproved of this behavior and, in an effort to shame him, they started calling him Jeff. But their plan backfired. His friends too began to call him Jeff. He must have liked it because years later, when he came to Missouri, he had his name legally changed to M. Jeff Thompson.

When "Jeff" was twelve years old, his mother died. At age fourteen he became a student at the Charlestown Academy, where the curriculum included not only the conventional subjects of Latin, Greek, English, and mathematics but also military training. He attended Charlestown Academy until he was seventeen. During his first year, he tried to volunteer for the navy of the Republic of Texas (which at that time was still independent of the United States), but of course he was turned down because of his age. The next year his father moved to Washington, D.C., and Jeff was left behind to board with a Mrs. Cramer. He applied for admission to the U.S. military academy at West Point but was rejected. During his third year at Charlestown Academy a brief but poignant diary entry notes, "Tried to get into Lexington Military Academy but H. Tucker Lee was appointed." What Jeff Thompson may not have known was that he lacked the political backing typically needed to get accepted into a military academy.

Even though Jeff's boyhood ambitions for a military career were frustrated for a time by these failures, his dreams never completely faded away as he grew into manhood. Still, for nearly four years after he left school, he drifted from job to job in various eastern cities—Charlestown and Shepherdstown, Virginia (now West Virginia), Philadelphia, and Baltimore. In 1846 he spent Christmas week in Frederick City, Maryland, and wrote in his diary that it was "the happiest week of my whole life." Too bad he didn't explain why.

In 1846 he decided to go west and took a job in Liberty, Missouri, clerking in a dry-goods store—which happened to be near another U.S. arsenal filled with arms and equipment. Surely, this must have reawakened childhood memories and dreams. It wasn't long before his employer entrusted him with a more exciting assignment than clerking—a chance to join an overland expedition carrying wagonloads of goods to the Rocky Mountains.

A new adventure began when he met a young woman named Emma Catherine Hayes, the daughter of a Baltimore artist who was taking his family to California. He married her on March 4, 1848, and the young couple made their home in St. Joseph, Missouri.

At the time, St. Joseph was the largest and most famous city in Missouri west of St. Louis. Its founder, the ambitious, adventurous Joseph Robidoux III, had first visited the site in 1779 as

Indian tribes turned over title to two million acres of what is now north-west Missouri to the United States in the Platte Purchase of 1836. Added to Missouri the following year, it was soon open to settlement, and the area, which the Native Americans had called the beginning of the road to paradise, rapidly attracted new settlers to what became Platte, Buchanan, Andrew, Holt, Atchison, and Nodaway Counties. Mural by George Gray, Pony Express National Museum, St. Joseph, Missouri. *State Historical Society of Missouri, Columbia.*

a sixteen-year-old apprentice to his father on a fur-trading expedition up the Missouri River. After his father's death he engaged in the fur trade with his brothers. At various times he was employed by the powerful Chouteau family's French Company; at other times he was competing with them and other St. Louis fur traders. Historian Tanis C. Thorne reports that Robidoux bought rights to the Black Snake Hills Trading Post in the early 1830s.

After Missouri obtained the Platte region in 1837 (despite the area having been set aside as a permanent home for the Indians in 1830), settlement in the area grew. Buchanan County, where St. Joseph is located, was formed in 1839. In the early 1840s the settlement had two surveyors, and Robidoux asked each of them to draw up plans for the town. Prussian surveyor Fred Smith drew a European town plan with narrow streets running toward the river. He suggested the town be named St. Joseph, for

Robidoux's patron saint, and named the proposed streets for members of the Robidoux family. His plan eventually won. By 1845, Jesuit missionary Pierre Jean De Smet reported that the "Americans, French, Creole, Irish, and German settlers had already built 350 houses, two churches, a city hall, and a jail," and declared the town to be in a "most prosperous condition."

Jeff Thompson went to work for Middleton and Riley, dealers in dry goods, hardware, and groceries. St. Joseph was teeming with fur trappers and traders, Native Americans, and, after President James K. Polk announced the discovery of gold in California in his annual address in 1848, gold-rush hopefuls on their way to California. The town also continued to serve as the departure point for fur traders such as Joseph Robidoux and his brothers, who sent caravans of heavily loaded wagons to the West and Northwest to trade for furs.

Thompson soon became part of this colorful scene, and in 1850 he led a wagon train to Salt Lake City, Utah. As he later related, the trip involved traveling over a vast territory, scarcely more than a wilderness, with almost no one living between the Missouri River and his destination. On the return trip his party was caught in a terrible snowstorm, but with his quick thinking and decisiveness he was able to lead the group safely down the Platte River and back to St. Joseph. He later boasted that the action he took to save the party was to draw his pistol and vow to shoot the first man who refused to keep moving.

Unfortunately, Thompson's notes on this expedition (now a part of the Southern Historical Collection, University of North Carolina at Chapel Hill), while intriguing, are not fleshed out. For example, he once wrote:

"Salt Lake City. Mormons. Wholesale trade. Remarks in the sermon about speculators. Visit to the Lake. Jump in."

He wrote again, later:

"Snow storm. I walk. Snow, snow."

Then, in a still later entry, he wrote:

"The last effort. The success. The ambulances. The mules. Frozen."

And finally:

"Start for home. The corn cache and whiskey. Cross on the ice at Plattesmouth."

Years later, John Schuder of St. Joseph wrote in a letter, "We can only sigh with regret for the loss of so interesting a narrative." He added, "A veritable epic of heroic adventure, worthy, as it stands, of the pen of [the poet] Vachel Lindsay."

Jeff had not lost his lifelong interest in the military; the attributes of a military leader were too deeply ingrained in him. Soon after his arrival in St. Joseph he joined the Missouri State Militia, a volunteer group, and enthusiastically supported all its activities. Before long he was commissioned as a colonel, and his popularity in the organization undoubtedly paved the way for the active role he would eventually play during the Civil War.

Jeff Thompson became one of the most prominent citizens of his adopted city of St. Joseph. In 1851 he went into the grocery business with a partner, but within a year that firm failed. Undaunted, Thompson signed on with a group of engineers who were conducting a preliminary survey for the Hannibal and St. Joseph Railroad. While on this job he gained a broad knowledge of practical engineering, which stood him in good stead the rest of his life. He had been hired originally as a commissary, but by the time the group returned to St. Joseph he was its leader.

Mark Twain, in his novel *The Gilded Age,* written with Charles Dudley Warner, draws on Jeff Thompson's legendary characteristics to poke fun at the post–Civil War era of rapid expansion and accompanying corruption. In the chapter "The Model Engineer: Survey to Stone's Landing," Colonel Sellers declares that Thompson "understands the wants of Stone's Landing, and the claims of its inhabitants. . . . Jeff says that a railroad is for the accommodation of the people and not for the benefit of gophers." As "one of the most enthusiastic engineers in this Western Country, and one of the best fellows that ever looked through the bottom of a glass," the authors wrote, "There was nothing that Jeff wouldn't do, to accommodate a friend, from sharing his last dollar with him to winging him in a duel."

When prospective investors in Stone's Landing visited the camp of the "redoubtable engineer" and enjoyed Thompson's hospitality, he demonstrated that "to drink from a jug with one hand was 'as easy as lying' . . . He grasped the handle with his right hand, threw the jug back upon his arm, and applied his lips to the nozzle. It was an act as graceful as it was simple, and as Jeff pointed out, 'it puts every man on his honor as to quantity.'"

After entertaining his visitors, Thompson retired to his tent to work on his field book, "then arose, stepped outside the tent door and sang, in a strong and not unmelodious tenor, 'The Star-Spangled Banner' from beginning to end. It proved to be his nightly practice to let off the unexpended steam of his conversational powers in the words of this stirring song." *The Gilded Age* was published in 1873, and when asked by a St. Joseph newspaperman about the book, Thompson explained that Warner, a surveyor, had worked on the survey for the Hannibal and St. Joseph Railroad.

While he worked for the railroad, Thompson became part of a group that laid out plans and promoted the growth of the new town of Hamilton, Missouri, in Caldwell County, thereby laying claim to becoming one of its founders. He was also assigned the job of supervising the construction of the western branch of the Hannibal and St. Joseph Railroad. When this was completed in 1857, Thompson went to Hannibal and rode the first train across the state. Shortly before the train arrived at St. Joseph, he mounted the engine and personally drove the first locomotive into the city.

Because Thompson had an enormous capacity for hard work and was liked by many in the community, his fortunes continued to rise. At one time, he served in at least nine responsible positions: he was mayor of St. Joseph, president of a newly formed gas company, president of the St. Joseph and Maryville Railroad, Buchanan County surveyor, real estate broker, Platte County Railroad agent, member of the Elwood Town Company, secretary of the St. Joseph and Louisiana Railroad, and colonel in the Missouri State Militia.

St. Joseph in the 1850s. Robidoux chose a city plan developed for the site of the Black Snake Hills post by a Prussian-born engineer, Fred Smith, who drew a European town with narrow streets running toward the river. Smith suggested naming the settlement St. Joseph, for Robidoux's patron saint, and named the streets for Robidoux family members. *State Historical Society of Missouri, Columbia.*

In this period of rapid growth and expansion of the western United States, Thompson played an important role as a surveyor of the first line for the Maryville Railroad and for part of the St. Joseph and Topeka Railroad. In addition, he surveyed large parcels of public land in Kansas and Nebraska for the U.S. government.

Because of his many and varied business interests, he traveled widely and became well known across northern Missouri. He also became active in political issues. When he was elected mayor of St. Joseph in 1859, he immediately mounted a vigorous campaign to make the city the major metropolis of the West—which involved laying out and grading streets, constructing bridges, and building a levee at the river to improve the harbor.

Jeff Thompson joined a group of engineers surveying the route for the Hannibal–St. Joseph railroad and in 1857 rode the first train across the state, driving it the last few miles into St. Joseph himself. This is a sketch of the first train on the Hannibal–St. Joseph line as it reached Chillicothe. *State Historical Society of Missouri, Columbia.*

The flood and erosion control plan he designed was so effective that it was used long after his death. He also drew up the plans for transporting the first locomotive across the Missouri River. Along the way, he even found time to conceive and develop several practical inventions such as a pistol lock, a brake for railroad cars, and a hemp breaker.

As Jeff Thompson prospered in the community, his family grew along with him. During the years in St. Joseph, his wife, Emma, gave birth to six children—Emma Catherine, Henry Bolivar, Mary, and Martha Washington, whom they called Marcie, survived. Two died in infancy. During this period, Jeff's sister Betty moved to St. Joseph and married John J. Abel, and his older brother Broadus and his wife also came to the city and settled there.

The Thompsons took an active part in St. Joseph's elegant social life. In 1859 Jeff managed an important ball and supper to celebrate the one hundredth anniversary of the birth of Scottish poet Robert Burns on January 25, 1759. Thompson was an

Thompson became active in business and social life in St. Joseph and was well known throughout north-west Missouri. *M. Jeff Thompson Papers, University of Missouri Western Historical Manuscript Collection, Columbia.*

honorary member of one of St. Joseph's early labor unions. And, although he was not religious himself, he chaired a Catholic benevolent society, perhaps to please his wife, who was Catholic.

In the two decades before the Civil War, Missouri became a blend of the South and the West, much like its eastern neighbors, Kentucky and Tennessee. Missouri had been admitted to the Union in 1821 with no restrictions on slavery. But unlike states in the Deep South, it had few large plantations with large numbers of slaves. The average Missouri slaveholder owned only four slaves. Most were either house servants, helped with general farming, or were rented out to supplement the family income. Slave owners lived side by side with those opposed to slavery.

Some of Jeff's friends and family members owned slaves, but he never did. Neither did he take part in the activities of politicians who tried to force a pro-slavery regime in neighboring Kansas. Because of that, he was sometimes accused of being soft

THE PONY EXPRESS
ST. JOSEPH, MISSOURI

On April 3, 1860, as mayor of St. Joseph, Thompson officiated as the first Pony Express rider set off from Pike's Peak Stables in St. Joseph with mail to Sacramento, California. On the return trip the riders brought mail from California to St. Joseph, where it traveled farther east on the Hannibal to St. Joseph Railroad. The Pony Express continued until October 1861, when telegraph lines to California were completed. Since 1980 the National Pony Express Association has sponsored a reenactment of the 1,966-mile ride from Sacramento to St. Joseph. *Photo of the Pony Express Monument, courtesy St. Joseph Museum.*

on the issue of slavery. But Thompson was a Southerner—by birth and by commitment. He believed the U.S. Constitution protected slavery, and he defended the rights of others to own slaves. He had an almost morbid fear of the emancipation of slaves, believing it would lead to racial war and bloodshed.

When he proclaimed, "There is but one great question now before the American people. It is the slavery question," he might have been surprised to know that a decade earlier his nemesis, Abraham Lincoln, had used similar language to declare his own conviction that slavery was "the one *great* question of the day."

When Thompson learned that the militant abolitionist John Brown and his band of twenty-one men had raided and seized the federal arsenal at Harpers Ferry, Thompson's birthplace, in October 1859, he left immediately for his home state to assess the situation for himself. Brown had been active in the violence between abolitionists and slaveholders in Kansas, and in an infamous incident a few years before, he and his sons had participated in the murder of five unarmed Southern white settlers. Thompson was deeply angered by Brown's attack on his childhood home. From that time on, he began to expect the worst from the North and to dedicate himself to rallying support for the Southern cause.

It was a distressing time for Thompson. He had lost money on his real estate speculations in Kansas and his political enemies were accusing him of accessing city funds for unauthorized railroad construction. While Thompson had served as county surveyor and later as mayor, he had mounted an extensive program of diking and strengthening the Missouri River shore to prevent erosion and flooding. He was also commissioned to sell municipal bonds to build a gas works and succeeded in selling them in Philadelphia, Baltimore, New York, and Boston.

These activities did not make him universally popular. He had his critics, some of whom felt his interest in river improvement was too closely linked to his railroad connections. John Glendower Westover quoted a letter published in the *Weekly West* of January 7, 1860, from one unhappy constituent:

> To His Majesty, M. Jeff Thompson, by the Grace of God,
> King of St. Joseph,
> Etc. Etc.

> May it please your Majesty: As the River Improvement is to
> be commenced on Monday next, I would suggest to your
> Majesty the propriety of first securing the warehouse of the
> Hannibal and St. Joseph RailRoad Co. and then continue the
> improvement upstream as far as the said company's prop-
> erty extends. Many of your Majesty's old subjects, who have
> placed you in the position you now occupy, are anxious to
> know if the property of the Hannibal, and St. Joseph
> RailRoad is entitled to more protection than that of the
> heavy taxpayers . . . Your subjects fear there is "something
> rotten in Denmark."

Moreover, many of Thompson's plans for railroad development were left uncompleted when he began to turn all of his
attention to the impending war.

When Jeff returned from Virginia, he announced that he
would not run for reelection. His last official act as mayor was to
preside at the ceremony to launch the Pony Express. On April 3,
1860, dressed in formal attire, he loaded the mail bags on a
prancing bay mare and bestowed the city's blessing on the first
west-bound Pony Express rider. In a speech he prepared for the
occasion, Thompson predicted, "The day will come when at this
very town you may board a train which will take you through to
the gold fields. Hardly will the cloud of dust which envelops the
galloping pony subside before the puff of steam will be seen
upon the horizon."

3

Prologue to War

In August 1860, in one of the most heated political contests in its history, Missouri elected Democrat Claiborne Fox Jackson, one of the largest slaveholders in Saline County, as its governor. According to many historians, Jackson won the election largely because he supported Stephen A. Douglas, the conservative Democratic candidate, in the campaign for president. The governor's election was a clear indication that Missouri did not favor the radical elements of either the North or the South; instead it chose the conservative middle ground. In the presidential election the following November, Missouri clung to that conservative attitude and cast its electoral votes for Stephen Douglas. Abraham Lincoln won the election.

As the possibility of war approached, most Missourians were not interested in fighting on either side. In fact most people would have liked to remain neutral. But not Jeff Thompson. When the news of Lincoln's election arrived in St. Joseph, he gave up all his other activities to focus on promoting the Southern point of view. In a pamphlet that he titled "An Address to the Citizens of the State of Missouri," he urged his fellow Missourians to prepare for war and call a state convention to consider secession from the United States. He concluded by saying:

> Therefore . . . if the Northern states that have passed laws
> nullifying the laws of Congress will not repeal them, if the
> majority of the people of the North insist upon waging a
> war of extermination upon us; if they continue to say we
> shall be hemmed in, and cut off, and finally driven into the
> Gulf of Mexico . . . if their own personal pecuniary interests
> will not stay their fanaticism and treason—then we must,
> for our own self respect, for our honor, for our fortunes yea,
> for our very lives, DRIVE THEM OUT OF THE UNION,
> and have a confederation of our own.

Aware that most German immigrants opposed slavery, Thompson warned all "native-born" Americans to be on guard, and he promised to blow his hunting horn at the first sign of danger.

When the Missouri legislature convened in January 1861, five states had either already joined South Carolina in seceding from the Union or were in the process of doing so. Thompson hurried to Jefferson City, arriving before January 1, to promote a military bill and to lobby for a secession convention. As he put it in his memoirs, he planned to "use my little influence to bolster up such weak-kneed and timid Southerners as might be frightened from doing right for fear that a war would be forced upon them." However, to his great disappointment, the military bill failed to pass and delegates to the secession convention, held in St. Louis, voted unanimously not to secede from the Union, although they did plan to meet again if circumstances warranted. Jeff left the state capital in disgust.

Having failed in his efforts, Thompson returned home, totally frustrated. When he got back to St. Joseph he learned that on April 12, 1861, Fort Sumter had fallen in South Carolina, making civil war almost a certainty. U.S. Secretary of War Simon Cameron had issued a call for troops. The new Missouri governor, Claiborne Fox Jackson, responded to that request on April 17: "Your requisition, in my judgment, is illegal, unconstitutional, and revolutionary in its object, inhuman and diabolical, and cannot be complied with." He called the Missouri legislature into special session and put the militia on alert. Thompson summoned his state troops to action, and on May 3, 1861, the militia encamped on grounds near the Patee Hotel.

In St. Louis large numbers of German immigrants, including some "48ers" who had fought for a failed revolution across numerous central European states in 1848, were strongly anti-slavery and pro-Union. Some formed guard units and drilled in anticipation of defending their new country. In early May, Governor Jackson ordered all state militia commanders to convene "Military Camps of Instruction." General Daniel Frost, who had framed the law that created the state militia, was commander of the First District, which included St. Louis. He established an encampment on the city's western outskirts, which he named Camp Jackson in honor of the governor. Frost and Jackson hoped to capture the large U.S. arsenal in St. Louis, and Jackson had written Confederate President Jefferson Davis asking for guns and munitions to carry out the attempt. Some arms did arrive from Baton Rouge, and Nathaniel Lyon, acting commander of the U.S. arsenal in St. Louis, decided to take action. Although he had sent the arsenal's arms and ammunition to Illinois for safekeeping, Lyon marched on Camp Jackson on May 10, 1861, took prisoners, and seized weapons and ammunition.

The militia company had surrendered without incident, but when word of the action spread, a large crowd gathered. As Lyon's men marched the prisoners back to the arsenal, violence broke out. His soldiers fired into the crowd, leaving at least twenty-eight civilians, including women and children, dead. This action came to be called the "Camp Jackson Massacre," and many Missourians blamed the Germans for the deaths. Jeff Thompson announced in Jefferson City that he had proposed a plan "to the Council of War" for "a speedy and bloodless peace." His tongue-in-cheek plan was to "burn all the breweries and declare Lager Beer to be a contraband of war. By this means, the Dutch [Germans] will all die in a week and the Yankees will then run from the state."

In St. Joseph, rumors began flying that Federal forces were

Abolitionist John Brown spent several years in Kansas in the late 1850s, participating in the civil war in the territories, and with his sons in May of 1856 carried out the infamous Pottawatomie Massacre, killing five unarmed pro-slavery settlers who lived near Dutch Henry's crossing at Pottawatomie Creek. When Thompson learned of Brown's raid on Harpers Ferry in October 1859, he impulsively left St. Joseph to go to Virginia to defend his birthplace. *State Historical Society of Missouri, Columbia.*

coming in from Leavenworth, Kansas, to capture the northwest Missouri state militia company in St. Joseph. On May 12, in a dramatic move, Thompson hastily commandeered wagons and, despite a raging thunderstorm, hauled away the camp equipment and powder from the city magazine where the weapons were stored, taking them out into the country. He sent half a dozen messengers across the countryside like latter-day Paul Reveres to summon Missouri patriots from their homes and shops to bring rifles, shotguns, and pistols. But it was a false alarm—no Federals came to disturb the new encampment.

When men arrived in answer to the call, there was no enemy to fight. Worse yet, Jeff was unable to get the governor's authorization to purchase food supplies, so the men had to go home hungry. This was only one event in a series of frustrations for Thompson that included having his house stoned. He finally decided to go home to Virginia and offer his services there—to "stand shoulder to shoulder with friends of my youth and strike for freedom."

On May 22, the day before he left town, he became embroiled in an incident that ended in his cutting down the U.S. flag from the roof of the post office. There had been so much excitement in St. Joseph about flying flags that the city fathers ordered that no more flags be raised. However, the newly appointed postmaster decided to risk raising the U.S. flag over the post office. When Thompson was asked if he would interfere with putting it up, he said, "No, put it up. It is none of my business." As he told the story later in his memoirs, when the flag was about to be hoisted, one of the post office employees invited Thompson to go with him for a drink, and he accepted. Then a second invited him to have a drink, and Thompson accepted that too. By the time the third invitation came, he realized that they were trying to distract him, but by now the flag was already up. Although he had advised everyone against taking any destructive action, he impulsively proceeded to climb the rope ladder that led to the roof and, amid cheers and jeers from the crowd that had gathered, cut down the flag. It fell into the street and was immediately torn to shreds. Later he wrote about the incident, apparently regarding it as a turning point: "I had cut down the flag that I had once loved. I had as yet drawn no blood from its defenders, but I was now determined to strike it down wherever I found it."

On his way East to join the Confederate cause, he stopped in Jefferson City once again. He asked to see the governor and was ushered into his office. Jeff described the emergency situation in St. Joseph and asked for assistance. Jackson was affable but would give no definitive answers. Finally Thompson gave up. "Governor," he said, "before I leave, I wish to tell you two

Jeff Thompson spent considerable time in Jefferson City in the early months of 1861, arguing for Missouri to leave the Union. *State Historical Society of Missouri, Columbia.*

qualities of a soldier—one of them he must have, but he needs both. One of them is common sense and the other is courage, and by God! You have neither of them." He turned on his heel and stalked out of the room.

Missouri was vitally important to both the Union and the Confederacy. The state's manpower pool, its strategic location on rivers and railways, its resources and wealth—these assets meant that Missouri was fiercely coveted by both sides, and it soon found itself a divided state in a divided nation. Many of its citizens were opposed to secession, and of those who supported the rights of states to secede, most believed that the states that left the Union eventually would return if left alone.

Governor Jackson hoped the North and South could find a way to preserve the Union. If that was not possible, then he wanted Missouri to join the Confederacy, but he had wanted the members of the state convention elected to consider secession to take the responsibility for the decision in the name of the people. In March this body had taken a wait-and-see approach, voting unanimously against leaving the Union but agreeing to meet again in December to reconsider. The December meeting never came to pass as hostilities escalated.

After Lincoln declared on April 15 that a state of "insurrection" existed and called for seventy-five thousand three-month military volunteers, the secession issue continued to be hotly debated. Except for his "Camps of Instruction," Governor Jackson had not done anything to openly support the South, although he continued to favor the Confederacy. Jeff Thompson tried openly, with florid proclamations and fiery speeches, to lead Missouri into the Confederacy. Pro-Unionists, however, were determined to keep Missouri in the Union and were willing to use force to ensure that it did not secede. Attempts by Governor Jackson and General Sterling Price to reach agreement with General Lyon and pro-Unionist Republican Congressman Frank Blair at a meeting in St. Louis on June 11 failed. Returning to Jefferson City, Jackson issued a proclamation and a call for volunteers, and Lyon set out from St. Louis with some two thousand troops to take Jefferson City.

Governor Jackson and key government officials left the capital on the steamer *White Cloud* and fled to Boonville with the Missouri state seal and many state documents, planning to set up a government-in-exile. After the state guard, led by a reluctant John S. Marmaduke at Jackson's orders, was defeated by Lyon's men at Boonville, Jackson went to the Confederate capital in Richmond, Virginia, to meet with Jefferson Davis. In late September he returned to Missouri to gather his family and slaves and flee south. Although Marmaduke's father remained loyal to the Union, John Marmaduke had decided to support the South. He resigned from the state guard to go to Virginia and join the Confederacy.

Meanwhile, the Missouri state convention, probably without legal authorization, convened, declared the state offices vacant, and named Hamilton Gamble as provisional governor and

Willard Hall as lieutenant governor. Many historians agree that Missouri owes a great debt to these men, especially Gamble, for their services. In spite of the determination of military officials to treat Missouri as a conquered state, Gamble used patience and moderation to organize a state government loyal to the Union that conservative citizens could support.

Jeff Thompson had traveled through southeast Missouri to Memphis, consulting with officials as he went. In Memphis he tried for a commission in the First Missouri Infantry Regiment, Confederate States of America, being formed by Colonel John S. Bowen. That effort failed, and hearing of Jackson's call for volunteers, he decided to return to Missouri. He first went to Pocahontas, Arkansas, and tried to recruit there with little success. When he learned that a meeting was being held at Martinsburg, Missouri, to organize a state guard battalion, he borrowed a horse, rode there, and was unanimously elected lieutenant colonel. Then, just a few days later, he learned that the First Military District of southeast Missouri was losing its general, and he was invited to stand for election. At first he demurred, but he soon allowed himself to be persuaded, especially when members of his battalion encouraged him to do so and promised to join him. He had purchased a white horse, which he named Sardanapalus, and on July 25, 1861, he headed for Bloomfield, Missouri, in Stoddard County. The men were assembling on Crowley's Ridge, a long strip of dry ground extending from Cape Girardeau almost to Helena, Arkansas.

When he rode into camp, he must have made quite an impression. As he reported in his memoirs, "I was dressed in a gray flannel shirt outside my pants, gray pants stuck into boot tops, a wool hat with a white plume in it, red sash, and a very large iron scabbard, sabre, pistol, and a bowie knife in my belt. I made altogether a rough appearance." Nonetheless, on the third ballot he was elected brigadier general, the rank he was destined to hold throughout the war. Following his election, when the question arose as to when he should take command, Thompson declared, "Tomorrow morning at guard mount, or not at all." That being agreeable, someone then called for a speech, so according to his memoirs, Thompson mounted a wagon and shouted:

> Soldiers of Southeast Missouri, you have elected me to the command of this district. I have no time to thank you. We have no time for idle words . . . I understand you want to fight. By God! You shall have it. I am a rip squealer, and my name is Fight.

4

The First Year of the War, 1861

Missouri! Missouri! Awake from thy slumber,
Hear'st thou not the hammer that rivets thy chains?
Can't the death shriek of fathers, the wail of thy mothers
The tears of thy daughters, arouse thee again?
Come! Rise in thy might, drive the Huns from thy borders,
And stand by thy Southern sons in the fight,
Pour forth all thy men, to help them to battle
For Freedom, for Glory, for Justice, for Right.
Let thy watchfires glow, and thy bugles blast high
O'er thy mountains and valleys, o'er the prairies and lea,
Then the glad shout shall ring o'er the prairies and streams,
Hail! Brothers Hail! Missouri is Free!

— M. Jeff Thompson, excerpt from "Appeal to Missourians,"
courtesy of the State Historical Society of Missouri, Columbia

I n the first year of the war, as he began his military career, Jeff Thompson faced many daunting challenges. Conditions in Missouri were critical. The governor had fled from Jefferson City and a provisional government had been appointed to replace the elected state officials. However, even though he had renounced the Union, Thompson's standing with the Confederacy was uncertain. His newly acquired rank of brigadier general was only with the Missouri State Guard, not with the Confederate Army, and his state troops were serving enlistment periods of varying lengths.

In addition to these important problems, Thompson even had a hard time keeping a suitable horse to ride. No ordinary horse was strong enough to keep up with his hard riding, and when he did obtain a good one, it was often stolen. In a war that was literally dependent on horsepower to carry couriers transporting orders or other military correspondence between officers who were often miles apart—or mule power to drag wagons loaded with military equipment and supplies or sick and wounded soldiers—these animals were essential to the war effort.

Still, despite all the problems he faced, Jeff was committed to the Confederacy's cause and willing to make great sacrifices to advance that cause. He was also ambitious for himself. In particular, he aspired to a commission from President Jefferson Davis as a full-fledged Confederate general. His native optimism and healthy ego made him certain that he could accomplish his goals.

Thompson's new command, the First Military District, stretched across southeast Missouri from Arkansas to St. Louis. Although strongly pro-Confederate in the southernmost counties, the area contained three major Federal posts—Cape Girardeau; Ironton, a mining center; and Bird's Point, a river landing opposite Cairo, Illinois—which was also enemy territory. Historian Frank Nickell and others have noted that "divided sympathies tugged at the social fabric" in Cape Girardeau. Many of its citizens were German immigrants who supported the Union. The presence of Missouri State Guards in the region led to the formation of four companies of Missouri Home Guard units, dominated by Germans, by July 1861. In addition, St. Louis, another important Union city, lay at the district's northern border.

Establishing his headquarters in Bloomfield, Thompson started by putting his men to work. Generals were normally

Many recent German immigrants to St. Louis, opposed to slavery and secession, formed Home Guard units to support the Union as tensions in the city grew. This drawing, with its Union Forever motto, is from John Buegel's Civil War Diary, begun in St. Louis in 1861. He wrote that "when the southern states, by capturing and destroying Fort Sumter, South Carolina, on April 13, 1861, declared open warfare with the northern states, the excitement in the whole country was tremendous. All work, indeed all trade and traffic, came to a standstill." *University of Missouri Western Historical Manuscript Collection, Columbia.*

After the capture of Camp Jackson, a state militia encampment in St. Louis, by federal troops on May 10, 1861, rioting broke out as the Union soldiers marched the prisoners toward the U.S. arsenal. When shots were fired, the soldiers, many of them German immigrants serving as Home Guards, fired into the crowds, killing twenty-eight civilians. The "Camp Jackson Massacre" enraged Jeff Thompson, and it was long and bitterly remembered by many in Missouri. *State Historical Society of Missouri, Columbia.*

appointed, not voted on in elections, but when regularly appointed General Nathaniel W. Watkins had resigned, his command had taken the unprecedented step of electing his successor themselves, and newly elected Jeff Thompson took his responsibility seriously. His first big job was to organize and equip his brigade, which consisted of approximately two thousand men—former state troops, not yet officially Confederates, who were poorly armed and equipped. Many men even made their own clothing from fabric distributed to them. It was frequently said, perhaps not entirely jokingly, that the standard equipment for a soldier in the Missouri State Guard was a quart of whiskey, a loaf of bread, a pocket Bible, a Barlow knife, and a fine-tooth comb.

The men set to work cleaning up the area, then pitching their tents on the freshly policed campground. Since most of them had no tents, Thompson taught them how to build temporary brush shelters. Next, he set about organizing and training his officers and drilling the troops to make them more soldierly. By evening, as a result of his efforts, he could honestly claim that "our camp *looked* like a camp."

He later ordered tents for those who did not have them. Apparently, he did not even have a tent for himself, because three weeks after he assumed command and after he had met with Confederate General Gideon Pillow in New Madrid in early August, he wrote a plaintive request to Pillow on August 17: "I herewith send you a requisition for a tent for my own use. I have been sleeping about, more like a stray dog than a general." He requested other necessary articles, such as boots, shoes, and soap for himself and his men. He also sought donations from civilians and, where necessary, gave orders to impress— take over—cattle, horses, wagons, corn, and other necessities, for which he always gave a certificate of indebtedness. These certificates were merely receipts for the value of the confiscated property, which were later redeemable in Confederate money or Missouri defense bonds that gave the owner a claim against the government-in-exile for the value of the property taken. Confiscating property by individual soldiers was not officially condoned, but Thompson realized that his troops must have certain items to fight a war.

Not surprisingly, some citizens protested having their horses or wagons taken and petitioned to have their possessions returned. It was Thompson's job to deal with each of these requests on a case-by-case basis. In his memoirs, he told of one man whose wagon and two horses had been impressed. Thompson knew that the old fellow still had several more wagons, as well as a carriage and an ambulance. The man

Thompson in one of the uniforms he put together during the months he spent in southeast Missouri and northeast Arkansas. *University of Missouri Western Historical Manuscript Collection, Columbia.*

presented himself as a Southern sympathizer, but Thompson had learned that he was planning to return to Kentucky to escape the war in Missouri. Engaging the man in conversation, Thompson convinced him that the army needed the wagons and horses more than he did and persuaded him to let the army keep them. Then Thompson went even further. He asked if the old gentleman could spare an ambulance and a pair of mules. The man apparently became convinced of the need and promised to send them along, much to Thompson's delight. But as the man left, Thompson reported, he warned others who were waiting their turn to complain not to go in lest the general coax them out of everything they had!

Despite his best efforts, Thompson's command continued to be poorly armed and equipped. He managed, however, to mislead the enemy by exaggerating his strength and by using tactics suitable to the swampy area in which he was operating. To that end, he set the engineer and his assistant to the crucial task of making detailed maps to show every county and town, every camp they made, every road, and every other bit of useful information. To emphasize the importance of these maps, he threatened to hang one of them if he found any important information had been omitted from a map or any errors had been added.

In early August Jeff had decided to ride south, through swamp and farmland, to New Madrid, the county seat of New Madrid County, to report to General Gideon Pillow, his immediate commander, and find out the plans for himself and his men. Pillow had landed there with his five-thousand-man "Army of Liberation" on July 28. When he arrived at Pillow's camp headquarters, Thompson was still wearing the outfit he had worn to Stoddard County for his election. As he looked around at the brilliantly uniformed officers, he realized he must look "wild and strange," as he put it. However, General Pillow received him warmly and seemed pleased with Thompson's eagerness to serve.

Lieutenant Governor-in-exile Thomas C. Reynolds was already there, and the next day Governor-in-exile Jackson arrived, having just returned from Richmond where he had obtained President Davis's agreement to help Missouri when it seceded. Although he was already suffering from cancer that would take his life the following year, Jackson's determination to deliver Missouri to the Confederacy had not faltered. On August 5 Jackson issued a "Proclamation of Independence," which, according to Christopher Phillips, Reynolds had written, declaring Missouri an independent and sovereign state. He was much encouraged by the Confederate victory over Union troops at the Battle of Wilson's Creek near Springfield, Missouri, on August 10, in which Union General Nathaniel Lyon lost his life.

Pillow and Jackson agreed that Thompson and General W. J. Hardee should collaborate in capturing Ironton. Thompson was

ordered to take his troops to Greenville, in Wayne County, where
General Hardee, who had moved into Missouri from northeast
Arkansas, would be. So the next morning Jeff returned to
Bloomfield where his men were waiting, arriving late in the
afternoon. Designating the route they would take and starting
for Greenville at dusk, he issued orders to march and, with no
respite for himself, rode all night and arrived in Greenville at
breakfast time.

When he met General Hardee for the first time, Thompson
was impressed by his plain speech and unassuming manner.
Hardee had come to Missouri intending to destroy the Iron
Mountain Railroad and defeat the Union forces at Pilot Knob.
However, while they were still meeting, a courier brought the
message that the railroad bridges had not been burned as
planned. Hardee then asked Thompson to undertake this operation. He eagerly agreed. He had high hopes of being part of what
promised to be a larger offensive that would include a strike on
Cape Girardeau. But, to his chagrin, the plan would ultimately
be scrapped when General Pillow wrote Thompson from New
Madrid on August 24 that he had a carbuncle on his seat and
couldn't ride a horse.

That afternoon, Thompson made arrangements for a forced
march to begin at dawn the next day. But at about midnight he
received new orders to return to New Madrid and report back to
General Pillow. Thompson was frustrated but set out the next
morning for New Madrid, and at dusk he met his infantry near
Mingo Swamp. It began to rain. Realizing that the rain would
make the swamp impossible to cross, he decided to leave that
night. He had his men make torches to light their way. Then
some eighteen hundred men, afoot and on horseback or in wagons, set off through the swamp. When they finally reached
higher ground, they lay down—in the rain—and rested until
morning. It had taken them six hours to make only three miles.
But Thompson was pleased to see that their spirits were still
high. As he told it, "No torch light procession, in the highest
political excitement, ever surpassed our night march through

Mingo Swamp." Historians believe it was after this night march that Jeff Thompson first began to be known as the "Swamp Fox of the Confederacy."

Clearly, Thompson reveled in this adventurous march, later writing in his memoirs, "We actually performed that night what I conceive to be the most original and brilliant thing which we did during the campaign." He also claimed that the clamor of the men shouting and calling for new torches or to be pulled out of the mud "made those forests echo in such style that the coons, the minks, and the owls . . . will hand down the accounts of their fright to the latest generation."

Over the next few weeks Thompson's men fought several skirmishes and won enough victories to give them a greater sense of confidence. In the first of these, Thompson sent part of his cavalry to the German settlement of Hamburg to pick up some arms that had been gathered and also to destroy an enemy fortification. The mission was successfully carried out, but with perhaps a bit too much zeal. As Thompson reported in his memoirs, "The temptation to have a brush before leaving was too great, and they charged into the town of Hamburg, scattering the Dutch in all directions."

Looting had begun to be a problem, as reported in St. Louis by the *Missouri Republican* on August 30, and Thompson took strong steps to keep his men from plundering civilians. He issued an order that any person other than a regular quartermaster responsible for supplies and equipment who took private property or was caught stealing horses would be hanged from the nearest tree. Eventually, he had to carry out this threat when a man admitted he had stolen a horse. He had at least three more men hanged for horse stealing, which, he maintained, stopped the practice.

Through the combined efforts of General Sterling Price in southwest Missouri, Hardee in southern Missouri, and Thompson in the Bootheel, the South was gaining ground in Missouri. Frustrated after the Union defeat at Wilson's Creek on August 10, Union General John Charles Fremont, newly arrived

General John Charles Fremont. Appointed commander of the Department of the West, the famous explorer arrived in St. Louis at the end of July and was soon overwhelmed by the growing unrest. He declared martial law, first in St. Louis and then in Missouri. His August 30, 1861, proclamation, in which he threatened to shoot all rebels, and confiscate property of Southern sympathizers and free their slaves, soon led President Lincoln to relieve him of his command. *Courtesy of Karlene Bessler from the collection of Vera Decker.*

Commander of the Department of the West in St. Louis, reacted by issuing a proclamation on August 30 declaring Missouri to be in a state of martial law. Fremont's proclamation was filled with threats against suspected Southern sympathizers. It included orders to shoot persons who were armed and to confiscate the property of those fighting the United States, including their slaves, who would then be freed. In a quick response, Thompson issued his own counterproclamation, swearing that he would "hang, draw and quarter a minion of Abraham Lincoln" for every man Fremont put to death. President Lincoln ordered Fremont to rescind portions of the proclamation, including the emancipation of slaves, as soon as he received it. A few months later Lincoln would relieve Fremont of his duty as commandant of the Department of the West, but Missouri remained under martial law.

Thompson had decided on a small offensive of his own. On

the last night in August 1861 he undertook a night expedition with a detail of 250 cavalry, a cannon, and three wagons. At nine o'clock in the evening they set out on a secret mission to Charleston, Missouri, a county seat within ten miles of Cairo, Illinois. The men traveled all night, crossing the swamp and several lakes, until at daybreak they were finally on dry ground north of town. Thompson had the cannon placed in front of the Bank of Charleston; then he rode to the home of the bank cashier. He called the cashier out and handed him a note, a copy of which is included in the book *Voices of the Swamp Fox Brigade: Supplemental Letters, Orders and Documents of General M. Jeff Thompson's Command 1861-1862*, edited by James E. McGhee. The note said:

> Demand on the Union Bank of Charleston
> Charleston, Mo., Sept. 1, 1861
> Sunday, 7:45 a.m.
>
> President and Directors of the Branch of Union Bank: Present Gentlemen: You have until 8:00 a.m. to determine whether I shall take possession of the funds in this jurisdiction, or whether your Cashier shall remove the same, books and all, to Bloomfield (under my charge) subject to further orders from the Commanding Officers of the Missouri State Guard.
>
> Yours respectfully,
M. Jeff Thompson
Brigadier General
Commanding

The distraught cashier asked if he could call the bank directors together so the full responsibility would not rest on his shoulders. Thompson agreed. Within an hour, a quorum was assembled. Thompson again stated his objective and gave the men fifteen minutes to decide whether they would give up the money peaceably, or whether he must take it by force. When the time was up, they informed Thompson that they would give it up, but under formal protest. He demanded the keys to the vault and took the bags containing gold and silver. The amounts marked on the bags totaled $57,000. Thompson gave them a receipt for that amount, but the bags later yielded only $56,000. In writing about the incident in his memoirs, he maintained that "the whole affair was conducted with dignity and politeness . . . I could not have conducted myself with more courtesy and respect toward them."

Most of the money was used to buy cannon, harnesses, salt, and other necessities for his army; the balance was put in a Memphis bank. Later on, Missouri's Governor-in-exile Jackson came to Memphis and censured Thompson for taking the money, but Thompson, when writing of this in his memoirs, insisted that Lieutenant Governor-in-exile Thomas Reynolds had approved the expedition beforehand. Jackson asked how much of the money was left. Thompson told him it was about $32,000. Jackson wanted to take it all, maintaining that the Confederacy should pay for major expenses, inasmuch as a million dollars had been allocated by the Confederate States Congress on August 6, 1861, to supply clothing, arms, ammunition, and other supplies for the Missouri troops. However, he finally agreed to compromise by taking three of the remaining four boxes of money and leaving one to pay for some outstanding small debts. Of course, the sly Swamp Fox, who knew the exact amount of money in each box, chose to keep the one that contained $27,000 in gold and gave Jackson the other three boxes, each of which contained only $1,200 in silver.

Shortly after the Charleston Bank raid, General Pillow decided to move his forces into Kentucky and invited Thompson to join him. Because he did not have the authority to order Missouri Guard members out of the state, Thompson called for volunteers, and most of his men chose to accompany him. They traveled by steamboat and reached Columbus, Kentucky, early in the morning. Even before they finished eating breakfast, they got word that Union gunboats were coming and were already preparing to land. Thompson and his men hurried to the ensuing battle, which was viewed by a large crowd gathered on the

Columbus bluffs to watch. It was not much of a skirmish, but it was important to Thompson because it was the first time he had actually been under direct fire. He confessed he was relieved to learn that he was able to stand up to it. After several shellings by the gunboats, however, General Pillow ordered Thompson to move to Belmont, across from Columbus, saying that "the place you are now is not safe."

Thompson replied, "I am not hunting safe places now." But he obeyed and withdrew.

Although he never said so directly, Thompson must have had a hard time trying to serve under Pillow because of the ill will between Pillow and General Leonidas Polk, who was Pillow's superior officer. The two constantly disagreed, and Thompson's brigade was frequently moved for offensives that were not carried out because orders were changed. On one such occasion he vented his anger by writing to General Benjamin Cheatham at New Madrid, "I know that the first duty of a soldier is to obey orders, but I will be very loth to turn back again." Despite his frustrations, however, Thompson managed to get along reasonably well with both Pillow and Polk, perhaps partly because his troops were state guard troops and owed their primary allegiance to Governor Jackson rather than directly to the Confederate generals.

Meanwhile, Pillow ordered Thompson to have his cavalry burn a large bridge on the Cairo and Fulton Railroad near Bird's Point and to have his infantry ready to support the cavalry. Thompson made up a detail of five hundred cavalry for the assignment and put a man identified in Thompson's memoirs only as Colonel Jones in charge of it. General Thompson realized that there would be resistance by the enemy and thus losses suffered by his men. He explained the whole operation to them and gave explicit orders concerning the passing of responsibility in the event of expected losses. "When Jones is killed," he said, "Smith will take command; when Smith is killed, Lewis will take command . . . and so on. But gentlemen, if there is but one man left at the end of the fight, he must burn the bridge!"

Thompson waited eagerly for a report from the detail. He knew the cavalry should reach the bridge by daybreak, so he anticipated a report by ten o'clock. But no report came. At noon there was still no report. He waited until late afternoon and, when a report still had not arrived, he sought out some of the infantrymen who had been the cavalry's backup support. He asked them if the bridge had been burned. They seemed surprised and said, "What bridge?"

When Thompson finally got hold of Colonel Jones, he demanded, "Why did you not report when you returned, sir?"

"I had nothing to report."

"Did you burn the bridge that I sent you to burn?"

"No sir."

"Why not, sir?"

"Because, sir, when I got up to about five miles of the bridge, I asked an old lady about it, and she said she had been down to the bridge and that there was a guard there and it would be dangerous to go there."

Thompson's careful plan had failed. According to his memoirs, he couldn't find words enough to express his indignation. He stopped his tirade only when he ran out of words and breath. Thompson later wrote that he had ordered Jones court-martialed, but in its "mistaken leniency" the court had only suspended him for twenty days. Westover reports that the bridge was eventually destroyed, reportedly with the assistance of the president of the railroad and the chief engineer.

It was time for a much-needed break for Jeff Thompson. Sometime in September he put in for a four-day furlough to go to Memphis, but General Pillow denied his request. Then, predictably, General Polk granted it, so Thompson was able to enjoy a brief respite in Memphis before returning to duty.

In his memoirs, Thompson recalled that one of the most "amusing" things that happened on his visit to Memphis was a stunt he arranged with his orderly, Ajax. Simon Martin, or Ajax, as Thompson called him, was described by Basil Duke as a "gigantic and truculent-looking Indian." Thompson was invited to a benefit "Tableau," and when he suggested his plan to Ajax, "He understood perfectly what I wanted done for he had been the proprietor of a showboat on the Mississippi River when the war began, and with brothers and sisters had been giving 'Tableaus of Ancient History'—Ajax delivering the lectures and explanations."

As the scene ended, "a confusion was heard at the door." "In stalked Ajax," and "with his most theatrical air handed me a letter." On this occasion Thompson read the letter, indicated it was nothing of importance, and asked Ajax to sit with him. "Little did that audience know," he wrote, "that I had arranged this little 'by show' for their entertainment. . . . There are hundreds who remember his war whoop in the Indian scene which came on soon afterward."

In late September 1861, Thompson was ordered to take his troops back into Missouri to make demonstrations and distract the movements of the enemy. A few weeks later the Missouri legislature-in-exile assembled at Neosho, in Newton County, at the call of Claiborne Jackson and there, perhaps without a quorum, voted on October 28, 1861, to secede from the Union. The Confederate Congress subsequently accepted Missouri into the Confederacy and added its star to the Confederate flag. After that, Confederate officers could legally give orders to Thompson and his men.

A short time later, while the enemy believed him to be elsewhere, Thompson planned and carried out the burning of the Big River Bridge. Because this severed connections between St. Louis and the railroad terminal at Ironton, the strike was effective, both psychologically and militarily.

Many years later, L. E. Jenkins, who was with Thompson's army, wrote of the events leading up to the battle and his experiences afterward:

> General Jeff Thompson, being in command of the Confederate forces in Southeast Missouri, moved his command by way of Marble Hill, through Bollinger and St.

Francis Counties to Colonel Jack Smith's residence just north of Big River mills. When near Libertyville, a number of citizens met us with loads of good things to eat. . . . They gave us a bountiful spread with some of the prettiest girls to wait on us. . . . My, Jeff was in his glory; naturally vain, a great admirer of ladies, a good talker. So after dinner, he made them a speech. After complimenting the dinner and the pretty girls he told them that his ragtag Missourians could whip their weight in wildcats. . . . He expressed an opinion then that I have often thought of. He said undrilled soldiers were the best fighters, the reason being . . . they did not know when they were licked, but the drilled soldiers knew. . . . as soon as the commander did.

Jenkins reported that the Big River Bridge was guarded on the east side by a fort on the bluff, manned by a company of Federal soldiers from Illinois. They were not expecting an attack. The guard was leaning on his rifle, watching the cook prepare breakfast when the attack came, and as Jenkins rushed into the fort, he saw the young guard lying dead.

After the burning of this bridge, a Union officer who had been taken prisoner by Thompson's men refused to give up his sword to his captors. The general asked him why. The officer replied contemptuously that Thompson's men were nothing but guerrillas, dashing over the countryside, burning bridges and murdering people—and that he refused to give up his sword to such persons. Although Thompson was in fact familiar with guerrilla tactics and used them when necessary, he keenly resented being tarred with the label of guerrilla. Guerrilla bands were not recognized by either side of the conflict. Thompson's force, however, was legally organized and recognized by Missouri and later by the Confederacy.

Very quietly, Thompson said to the Union officer, "My dear Sir, I am sorry to differ with you. I think we are soldiers and damned good ones . . . but you shall certainly have your choice of the kind of men you wish us to be." With that, he called his orderly, who enjoyed drama as much as Thompson did, and

Map showing southeast Missouri in 1860. *State Historical Society of Missouri, Columbia.*

said, "Ajax, that gentleman wishes to be treated as guerrillas treat their prisoners. Accommodate him."

When Ajax dismounted, dramatically drew his tomahawk, and advanced threateningly on the unfortunate Union officer, he hastily gave up his sword. This was only one of several occasions when Thompson used Ajax to frighten or trick others into believing his orderly was in reality a "savage Indian."

Union General John M. Schofield later wrote that because the destruction of the bridge at Big River disrupted communication with St. Louis, "in the nervous condition of the military, as well as the public mind at that time, even St. Louis was regarded as in danger."

Thompson's men continued to be poorly equipped. Few had uniforms, and some were even without shoes. But on October 21 about twelve hundred troops—who were outnumbered three to one by the enemy—fought valiantly in the battle of Fredericktown in Madison County for nearly three hours before retreating—taking with them about eighteen thousand pounds of lead from Mine La Motte, just north of Fredericktown. Officers and men on both sides fell in the fray—Thompson reported sixty men killed, wounded, or missing, and the Federals reported six killed and sixty wounded. Although defeated, Thompson and his men felt a sense of pride in what they had achieved, and some historians believe that actually neither side was victorious in this battle. In fact, as Jeff commented in his memoirs, "The enemy claimed Fredericktown as a great victory for them, but they are welcome to all such victories, for I, with 1176 poorly equipped men, had fought 9000 of their best men."

The next confrontation with the enemy—the battle of Belmont, at the steamboat landing opposite Columbus, Kentucky—took place on November 7. This engagement pitted Confederate forces against those of Union General Ulysses S. Grant, who was already under specific orders to capture Thompson. According to Grant's memoirs, he had received "important special instructions" from General Fremont, which Grant said assigned me to the command of the district of south-east Missouri, embracing all the territory south of St. Louis in Missouri, as well as all southern Illinois. At first, I was to take personal command of a combined expedition that had been ordered for the capture of Colonel Jeff Thompson, a sort of independent or partisan commander who was disputing with us the possession of south-east Missouri.

According to plans, when Grant arrived in Cape Girardeau, several troop reassignments in the area were to take place and after Thompson was captured, Grant was to proceed to Cairo. Meanwhile, General Benjamin M. Prentiss, who had been in charge of military operations in the area, had been to Ironton and had left most of his men at Jackson and come on to Cape Girardeau with a column of cavalry. Grant ordered him back to Jackson, "but he was very much aggrieved at being placed under another brigadier general." Prentiss went back to Jackson, as ordered, but "bade his command adieu and went back to St. Louis and reported himself. . . . He was sent to another part of the state."

This broke up the expedition to find Jeff Thompson, and Grant moved to Cairo on September 4. But as he wrote, "little harm was done, as Jeff Thompson moved light and had no fixed place for even nominal headquarters. He was as much at home in Arkansas as in Missouri and would keep out of the way of a superior force." In early November, Grant embarked from Cairo on transports with four thousand Federal soldiers. Heading downriver, they landed at Belmont and marched toward the Confederate camp. Grant wrote that he did not intend to have a battle but merely wanted to make a demonstration. The men, however, were tired of drilling and attacked the Confederates, who took advantage of the woods and marshlands and fought for four hours before retreating. The Federals considered the battle won, but when Confederate reinforcements came from across the river they retreated to their transports. The Union lost 480 men and the Confederates 642.

THE STARS & STRIPES

THE UNION. IT MUST AND SHALL BE PRESERVED

The first issue of *Stars and Stripes* was printed in Bloomfield, Missouri, in 1861. Union soldiers, hoping to capture Thompson, arrived after he had departed, but several Illinois printers among the soldiers produced the first issue of the paper in the abandoned newspaper office. The Stars and Stripes Museum in Bloomfield owns one of the three known copies of the first issue. *State Historical Society of Missouri, Columbia.*

According to historian Diana Lambdin Meyer, after the Belmont battle an Illinois infantry regiment that had been stationed in Bird's Point, an Iowa regiment in Cape Girardeau, and forces from Ironton arrived in Bloomfield, ordered by Grant to drive Thompson's forces from the town. "It was one of sixteen times during the Civil War that the little town of Bloomfield switched hands between the North and the South," Meyer wrote in the October 2005 issue of *Missouri Life.* The editor of the *Bloomfield Herald* had left town with Thompson's men, and by the morning of November 9, 1861, men from the Illinois regiment who were printers produced a newspaper, which they called *Stars and Stripes,* in honor of the American flag. They chose as the motto "The Union: It must and shall be preserved."

As winter approached, Thompson's men, who were still suffering from shortages of clothing, shelter, and medical supplies, began to fall prey to measles and other diseases. As a result, during November and December 1861 he lost more men than in the whole time since he had taken command of the brigade. No doubt, in addition to these health issues, many recruits were ready to avail themselves of the terms of Governor Gamble's amnesty proclamation of August 3, which would permit those "who had taken up arms against the government at the call of Governor Jackson" to take the oath of allegiance and return to their peaceful pursuits. Westover found that newspapers frequently reported on the great number of deserters from

Thompson frequently visited New Madrid, conferring with Confederate officers as to how his Swamp Fox Brigade could best assist in the war. Confederates built a Fort Jeff Thompson at New Madrid in late 1861. *State Historical Society of Missouri, Columbia.*

Thompson's command, and Thompson wrote, "When I was at Belmont my men got into the bad habit of leaving without permission," some returning again, and some deserting. Before the battle at Big River Bridge he determined that an example had to be made. "An old offender, named Smith, was brought into camp. He had deserted several times, and was said to have induced others to do the same." Thompson ordered a court-martial. It took several courts before Smith was sentenced to death. In spite of pleas from his men and from Smith, Thompson ordered him executed by a firing squad. Thompson wrote of the execution as "a great assumption of authority and a most terrible responsibility, but I thought, and still think that it was right."

On November 16, hoping to persuade two thousand of his men to reenlist for the war, Thompson wrote to General Sterling Price, reminding him that his men's six-month term of service was about to expire and seeking instructions for transferring his command into formal Confederate service. According to Westover, Thompson "sent repeated inquiries" to Price "and others to determine the correct procedure but received little attention."

In November a decision was made, over Thompson's objections, to build a fort at New Madrid. They named it "Fort Thompson." In his view, it would have been better to keep the enemy wondering where he was than to build a permanent fortification that would not be strong enough to withstand the Union force. As it turned out, he was right. Built with the labor of five hundred slaves, as Thompson wrote in his memoirs, "neither I nor the fort ever had any luck" from the day of its christening. The fort would be evacuated in March of the following year.

As the final expedition of the year, Thompson called for volunteers to carry out a raid on two clothing stores in the town of Commerce on the Mississippi River. They arrived on the Sunday after Christmas and demanded that the stores be opened. Thompson ordered a suit of clothes for each of his men, along with an itemized bill to be presented to the Confederacy for payment. As Thompson reported in his memoirs, "This was my Christmas gift to the men, and the eventful year of 1861 went out with this adventure."

5

The War Continues, 1862-1863

~

Come comrades open wide your eyes, and listen while I sing;
I'll promise that you'll shed no tears, about the news I bring,
For all seems bright and hopeful too, in our fair Southern land,
And all that we now have to do is keep our gizzards full of sand.
For we of all the noble hosts, that strikes for Southern Rights
Need patience more, and suffer most being kept away from fights
Where Glory Honor and our hate would sweeten every blow,
While all we do is DAMN THE FATE that will not let us go.

— M. Jeff Thompson, "Damn It, Let It Rip," Thompson memoirs

As the war went on, Jeff Thompson's goals continued to be to fight for a Confederate victory and, in so doing, to distinguish himself as a courageous military leader. He especially aspired to a commission as a brigadier general—or even beyond—in the Confederate Army.

But the winter of 1861-1862 at the New Madrid winter quarters could not have been an easy one for him. For some time he had been struggling to hold his force together while the enlistment period for most of his men was ending. As the new year of 1862 began, the numbers of his followers were greatly reduced, as many of the Missouri State Guard members volunteered for regular Confederate units.

In January 1862, on a trip to New Orleans, Thompson became acquainted with Confederate Major General Mansfield Lovell, who, he reported, "was not much older than myself . . . not much smarter." This encouraged him to think he really could become a general in the Confederate Army.

While Thompson was in New Orleans, exiled Governor Jackson gave him a hundred thousand dollars in Missouri bonds to pay his men for their services prior to November 1, 1861. Thompson returned to New Madrid on January 14, 1862, and began to distribute the money the next day. At about this time he was relieved of his command at the New Madrid post, and he wrote, "I had nothing to do now but to recruit for the Confederacy and settle my Brigade business and run about the country."

On January 22 he wrote from Missouri State Guard headquarters in New Madrid to Colonel Leonard Ross, Union commander at Cape Girardeau, asking if he would allow the "charitable citizens of Cape Girardeau" to contribute clothing to his men who were held in prison there. A few days later he wrote to Colonel Kitchen at Clarkton, offering his help to defend the plank road, promising "to hold this end against the devil."

In February he traveled to Richmond to talk to Jefferson Davis about securing his hoped-for commission. The Confederate president invited Thompson to meet with him at his home, but when Thompson arrived at the appointed time he learned that Davis was suffering from an ailment that was eventually to cause him to lose an eye, and could not meet with him. Confederate forces were withdrawing from positions in Bowling Green and Columbus in Kentucky and Nashville in Tennessee, so he wrote a note to Davis saying, "I came all the way to Richmond to see Jefferson Davis and let him see Jeff Thompson. But as the campaign has opened in the West, I must return to my post." He assured Davis "that I would fight under anybody, over anybody, any where and any how that he might direct." The next day he left for Columbus, having been in Richmond only thirty-six hours. In May he received a letter from Davis expressing

Union General John Pope captured New Madrid in March 1862, and in April, Island Number 10 fell. *State Historical Society of Missouri, Columbia.*

regret that he had been unable to see Thompson and adding that he required "no assurance" of Thompson's patriotism or bravery.

Back at Columbus, Thompson found the Confederate officers discouraged, ill, and dispirited from recent defeats. Wanting to brighten everyone's spirits, he took a few men and set out on a typically foolhardy expedition. Union General John Pope and his men were expected to march on New Madrid any day, and Jeff's plan was to delay their advance long enough to allow the state legislature-in-exile to have a meeting there.

His small party put on a demonstration near Sikeston, firing cannons and trying to trick the enemy into thinking they were a large force. But it didn't work. He soon learned that the enemy was well aware of his position and strength. When the order came for the Union troops to charge and capture him, Thompson was forced to retreat.

A running fight and a sixteen-mile race ensued, with a thousand Union soldiers giving chase to Thompson and his small band. Jeff called this retreat between Sikeston and New Madrid "the Sikeston races" and boasted that it was run in less than an hour. "We swept along," he said later, "shouting, yelling, cheering, damning, and even laughing, and we could have thought it royal sport . . . had not an occasional whizz, thug, succeeded by a groan or exclamation of pain, taught us that it was men playing war and playing for keeps at that."

Some of the Federal officers seemed to enjoy the chase as much as Thompson claimed he did. A member of the Seventh Illinois Cavalry wrote, "Then the fun commenced. We chased him for fifteen miles over a straight, wide, level road which he strewed with blankets, guns, hats, and at last his artillery." According to reports, one of Jeff's company was killed, two wounded, and six captured.

Ironically, for all his efforts, the proposed legislative session that Thompson had hoped to protect never took place. In addition, the Mississippi River flooded, overflowing banks on both sides from Island Number 10 to Cairo, sweeping away houses, trees, and everything in its way and making life miserable for both Union and Confederate forces in the area.

As Thompson wrote in his memoirs, when the Battle of Elkhorn Tavern was lost, "dark and ominous shadows" began spreading across the West. This battle, also known as the Battle of Pea Ridge, was fought March 6-7, 1862, in Arkansas. Confederate Generals Earl Van Horn, Ben McCulloch, and Sterling Price attacked and were repulsed by Union forces. In his book *Borderland Rebellion: A History of the Civil War on the Missouri-Arkansas Border*, Elmo Ingenthron calls the battle the second act of "an historic two-act drama," following the Battle of Wilson's Creek as the opening act. In this battle, as in Wilson's Creek, the contestants were so evenly matched that the victor, the Union, suffered equally with the vanquished, who did not admit they had been defeated. Nevertheless, the outcome of the battle disrupted Confederate plans to take St. Louis or regain Missouri.

During the next month or so, Thompson moved around even more than usual in his search for Confederate General Earl Van

Dorn, who commanded the area west of the Mississippi. Jeff wanted permission from Van Dorn to enlist recruits and mobilize at Helena, Arkansas, at the lower end of the great series of swamps and bayous. He recalled in his memoirs that in one thirty-day period he traveled 850 miles by steamboat, 130 in a dugout canoe, and more than 400 on horseback, for a total of nearly 1,400 miles, or almost 50 miles a day—and that he well deserved the name of "ubiquitous Jeff Thompson" given him by Union General Ulysses S. Grant. Considering the slow progress of a dugout and the long hours spent in a saddle, that was indeed an achievement.

In late March he finally overtook Van Dorn, who was on a steamboat heading for Des Arc, Arkansas, and got the permission he sought. He reported, "I found General Van Dorn very kind to me, and he immediately granted my most earnest desire, which was to remain in the Trans Missouri Department with all the men I could raise, and give the Enemy all the trouble that I could." He set to work and soon mustered four companies of infantry and three batteries. By now General Grant had fought and won the Battle of Shiloh in Tennessee, and the Confederate forces were in retreat toward Mississippi. In early April New Madrid had fallen to the enemy and Island Number 10 had been lost. In his book *The Bootheel Swamp Struggle,* Marshall Dial wrote that this defeat "started a rip that was to tear the Confederacy apart along the seam of the Mississippi."

On May 10, 1862, the first anniversary of the Camp Jackson Massacre, Thompson took part in the battle on the Mississippi River at Plum Run Bend in Tennessee. According to Richard Schroeder in *Missouri at Sea,* the Confederate Army's "Mississippi River Defense Fleet," eight rams "clad in protective bales of cotton" and "commanded by Captain James Montgomery and Missouri guerrilla Jeff Thompson," surprised the Union fleet and managed to sink the *Cincinnati.* The battle lasted only half an hour and ended in a Confederate retreat, although the Union flotilla suffered a real setback. "Montgomery bragged that the Union will never penetrate farther down the Mississippi

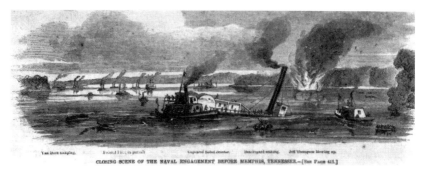

CLOSING SCENE OF THE NAVAL ENGAGEMENT BEFORE MEMPHIS, TENNESSEE.—[See Page 441.]

Camped near Memphis, Jeff Thompson and his men participated in the effort to keep the Union from gaining control of the Mississippi River. Serving on a Confederate ram, the Horse Marines, led by Thompson, were credited with winning the battle at Plum Run. But he later watched from the Memphis bluffs as the Confederate cotton-clads, including the one named for him, were destroyed in June 1862. In the Battle of Memphis on June 6, 1862, the CSS *General M. Jeff Thompson* was set afire by the guns of the Union warships, ran aground, and blew up. *Naval Historical Center, Courtesy Richard E. Schroeder.*

River," but less than a month later Memphis was captured by the Union forces. A weary and heartsick Thompson and his men managed to escape in the first train out of the defeated city. At the railway station he and his aides loaded their horses into an empty stock car and, at knife point, ordered the near-est trainman to attach the car to a train. Then the Missourian who had held the throttle on the first train into St. Joseph rode the first train out of stricken Memphis. He had watched the destruction of the frail Confederate cotton-clads from the shore and was quoted as saying, "They are gone, and I am going," as he mounted his horse and "left the citizens of Memphis to the Union Army." This was surely Jeff Thompson's lowest point of the entire war. He even considered quitting the war altogether. But he reconsidered when he learned that the Confederate Congress had authorized the establishment of Partisan Rangers in Mississippi, and that he was to have the job of mustering them.

After Memphis had fallen to the Union, Thompson was transferred to Ponchatoula, Louisiana. Although at the time he had only two hundred men at his disposal, he began to circulate the boast that he was going to enlist local support and capture New Orleans with at least ten thousand men. The much-despised General Benjamin Butler, known as "Beast Butler" for his harsh rule of the city, had occupied New Orleans since May 1. But even Jeff was surprised at the success of his deception—he wrote that "to my astonishment, Butler actually believed me, and evacuated Baton Rouge." The Federal troops withdrew from the Louisiana capital and went to New Orleans to reinforce General Butler.

Because Thompson was such a constant irritant to the Union forces, from General Grant on down, frequent attempts were made by the Federals to capture him, and he took delight in eluding them. Another of these narrow escapes occurred while he was in Austin, Mississippi. During the night, someone informed the enemy of his whereabouts, and troops were dispatched to take him prisoner. Before daybreak, a servant came to warn him that there was a steamship at the nearby landing. Thompson quickly got dressed, went outside, and ran for his horse, shouting to his men to mount. He jumped the fence and fled, not thirty yards ahead of his pursuers. He hadn't even had time to throw his saddle bags over his horse, but fortunately a servant girl retrieved them and sent them to him a few days later.

Thompson continued his efforts to achieve an appointment as a brigadier general in the Confederacy, writing in May to General Beauregard to ask him to forward his request for a commission. Instead, Beauregard endorsed the letter with the words, "I know no one whose zeal, energy, intelligence and daring is more worthy of a Brig," and returned it. Disappointed, Thompson nevertheless sent Beauregard's endorsement on to President Davis, who wrote on the back of Thompson's message the terse comment, "Referred to Sec. of War. J. D. File." Once again—no action.

In early July 1862 Thompson got the news ahead of the Union Army in Memphis that General Robert E. Lee had driven General George B. McClellan's Union Army away from the Confederate capital in Richmond in the Seven Days' Battles. From his location, he could hear Grant's cannon firing to celebrate Independence Day, and he immediately sent Grant a note saying, "We have neither whiskey nor ice to have a very gay celebration today, neither have we powder to waste, but the news from Richmond makes us jovial enough." His note was later published in Memphis newspapers and called "a piece of Jeff Thompson's impudence."

Meanwhile, in spite of moments of fame, Jeff was fighting battles, coping with military challenges, and avoiding capture. He was also faced with personal problems. Early in 1862 he had received disturbing news from St. Joseph. His home had been ransacked and vandalized by men who called themselves soldiers. His wife, Emma, was so upset by this that she fled to St. Louis, leaving their children behind with relatives. While in St. Louis, she, along with two other women, was arrested for being a Southern sympathizer and held for a few days in the female quarters of Gratiot Street Prison. When she was released, Jeff tried to make arrangements to have her join him, but for some time his efforts were to no avail.

Every time he tried to arrange for his family to come through the lines for a visit, Union General Henry Halleck refused them permission. But finally Jeff learned that, with the help of personal friends, a permit had been obtained. His family traveled to Memphis and from there to Canton, Mississippi. He immediately went to Canton to be reunited with his wife and their three oldest children, from whom he had been separated for nearly two years.

During one of Emma's visits, Thompson took her with him to Richmond to see President Davis about his commission. He had written the president earlier making formal application for a commission as a brigadier general. Now he was told that in order to obtain the commission, he needed either the backing of a member of the Confederate Congress or an immediate commanding general—or evidence that he had been able to form a new brigade of Missourians. Thompson did not have the necessary political support for a congressional or other recommendation, but he was confident—probably overconfident—that he could raise a brigade.

On December 5, 1862, he wrote President Davis once again, declaring that he had already recruited three thousand men— probably an optimistically inflated number—and that "more are coming in daily." The new secretary of war, James A. Seddon, recommended Thompson's appointment, but Davis, who despised guerrillas and did not want to use them in his army, may have seen Thompson as almost a guerrilla himself. In any case, Davis was skeptical of Thompson's recruiting claims and, after getting a report from his adjutant general's office that "nothing is known of this brigade," the president simply ordered that the request—which was the last one Thompson would make—be filed. End of story.

However, long after Thompson's death, when his oldest daughter, Emma Catherine, would write to inquire of Jefferson Davis why her father had not been commissioned as a Confederate general, Davis would respond by writing:

> Yours of the 16th Inst. was duly received and appreciated as coming from the daughter of a gallant soldier of the Confederacy. The only reason why your father was not a commissioned officer of the Southern Confederacy was that the troops he commanded were organized under the laws of Missouri and never mustered into the Army of the Confederacy, though cooperating with the efforts to maintain the inherited sovereignty and independence of the states.

After their visit to Richmond, Jeff and Emma returned to Jackson, Mississippi, where they had left their children with friends. Jeff made arrangements to send his two older daughters to a convent school in Louisiana and took his wife and son to Camden, Arkansas. From there he went on to Little Rock, the

Gratiot Prison in St Louis. Both Emma Thompson and M. Jeff
Thompson were imprisoned here. The building had been McDowell
Medical College, established by Dr. Joseph McDowell, an outspoken
Southern sympathizer. Dr. McDowell and one of his sons had managed to make their way to southeast Missouri with a personal arsenal that included two cannons in August 1861. *State Historical Society
of Missouri, Columbia.*

headquarters of the Trans-Mississippi Department, where he
was "received with a great deal of courtesy and kindness and
invited to speak to the state legislature." But as he wrote in his
memoirs, "I now made a grand mistake by accepting the invitation, for when I talk I am apt to say more than prudence would
dictate." In his speech, he criticized the leadership of the Western

Department and, as a consequence, he was not allowed to recruit troops in Missouri or Arkansas. As he told it, "I lost a command for 8 months and suffered 8 months' hardships and dangers without glory or thanks." He spent the next several months serving as an adviser on several expeditions in Missouri and Arkansas.

On January 1, 1863, Jeff Thompson left Pocahontas, Arkansas, for Little Rock where he again met his wife and son, who had come from Camden. He remained in Little Rock for most of January. But he found himself becoming depressed by the gloomy war news—Confederate forces in Prairie Grove, Arkansas, had been defeated, and many of his good friends fell in the battle. On January 7 the Arkansas Post was captured and the whole state became filled with stragglers and deserters. On January 22, trying to celebrate his birthday—or perhaps to forget the bad war news—Jeff drank so much whiskey that it made him sick, and he resolved not to touch another drop of liquor until the war ended—a vow that he kept.

In the early days of 1863, Thompson continued in his pattern of what he called "playing talent." He would mislead and harass the enemy by such means as "leaking" information that he was about to attack a fort when he was really planning to leave the area instead, or by building a breastwork—an improvised temporary fortification—to enable his small band to fight for six hours against the enemy's much larger force and not suffer a scratch while doing so, or, in another foray, by capturing sixty horses and taking twenty-three prisoners.

In April 1863 Thompson joined up with General John S. Marmaduke, who had led five thousand troops on an invasion into Missouri from central Arkansas starting on December 31, 1862. Marmaduke was now retreating southward, with the Federals in pursuit. Thompson offered to guide them safely through the swamps, and Marmaduke gladly accepted. However, the only escape route was by crossing the St. Francis River—and no bridge was available. Knowing of Thompson's experience as a civil engineer and of his wartime exploits,

Marmaduke asked him if he could build a temporary bridge. At once Thompson and a detachment of men went to work constructing a makeshift "floating" bridge while, in what was called the Battle of Chalk Bluff (May 1-2, 1863), Marmaduke managed to hold off the enemy until dark. Then, under cover of darkness, the artillery and wagons were pulled across the river on the fragile bridge. The men crossed in single file, while the horses were driven into the water and forced to swim across. Unfortunately, in the confusion, many saddles turned or slipped back on the horses' hindquarters, causing the horses to drown.

Finally, after everyone was across, the men cut the bridge loose and let it float away. An hour later, when the Federals reached the river, not a trace of evidence remained to show the enemy how the escape had been made.

During the latter days of May that year, Thompson learned that his wife and son, who had returned to Missouri, were again at Little Rock, so he "at once started to bring them up on the Ridge, where I could see or hear from them and probably provide for them when so far away and among strangers." After the visit, he arranged for a train and wagon to take his family on to Jonesboro.

In August the Missouri governor-in-exile Thomas Reynolds, who had taken office when Governor Jackson died in December 1862, issued orders authorizing M. Jeff Thompson to recruit a brigade in Missouri. It was a dangerous assignment because Thompson would often be behind enemy lines. But Jeff thrived on danger, and he immediately began the process. Then, on the afternoon of August 22, 1863, while he and two companions were working on their military maps in a hotel in Pocahontas, Arkansas, they suddenly heard horses approaching, and one of the men, Captain Reuben Kay, yelled, "By God, here's the Feds."

Thompson gasped in dismay but quickly collected his wits and ordered, "Kay, burn those maps." He immediately began to tear the maps into small pieces, which Kay then burned in the kitchen stove before the Union officers came inside. One of their captors was Captain Henry C. Gentry of Marion County, Missouri, the son of the president of the Hannibal and St. Joseph Railroad. After the initial shock, Thompson accepted his capture with dignity and good humor, which remained his demeanor throughout his imprisonment. He and the other prisoners were taken by train to St. Louis and on to the Gratiot Street Prison, probably arriving on August 24. The prison was in the former Missouri Medical College, founded by Dr. Joseph Nash McDowell in the 1830s. McDowell, a Confederate sympathizer, had departed St. Louis in 1861 with his son Drake and arrived at Jeff Thompson's camp in southeast Missouri in August of that year with two cannon and other arms.

The prison's main problem was overcrowding. The main building was eight-sided and built of gray stone with arched and square windows and flanked by two wings. Although equipped to handle five hundred prisoners, by November 1862 it already held eight hundred. The inadequate facilities meant that inmates were fed only two meals a day. Moreover, the crowded conditions made it easy for illnesses to spread, and many died from lack of medical attention. Thompson found a number of acquaintances among his fellow prisoners and was allowed to visit some of his own men who were in the hospital there. When required to fill out a questionnaire concerning his role in the rebellion, Thompson did so in his usual forthright manner. To the question, Are you a Southern sympathizer? he answered, "Decidedly." When asked, Do you sincerely desire to have the southern people put down in this war, and the authority of the U.S. Government over them restored? he responded, "No! Never!"

While he was in the St. Louis prison, Jeff's sister and brother-in-law made the journey from St. Joseph to visit him and brought his three-and-a-half-year-old daughter Marcie, whom he had not seen for more than two years. At the prison the visitors were roped off from the prisoners, but Marcie's uncle whispered to her, "When you see a big man hold out his arms to you, run under the rope, jump into his arms and slip this picture into his pocket." The "picture" was a hundred-dollar bill. When the tall man—whom Marcie did not remember—beckoned, she

"Our Mess," a sketch of the Confederate Officer's Mess at Johnson's Island, June 1864. M. Jeff Thompson, second from right, seated. *Courtesy of Missouri Historical Society Archives, Civil War Collection, Box 137.*

obediently ran to him, jumped into his arms and put the picture in his pocket while Jeff buried his face in her shoulder and sobbed.

After a few days at the Gratiot Street Prison, Thompson was transferred, probably around September 1, to the U.S. prison at Alton, Illinois, just across the river from St. Louis. While he was there, a man named George Prentiss wrote to the military command at St. Louis, saying:

> I learn that General M. Jeff Thompson is in the prison at Alton, Illinois. A year and a half ago, while he had a command in Arkansas, he did me a kindness by writing to me information in regard to my son. I hope you will not deem it inconsistent with your public duty to permit me to send him a demijohn of whiskey. Please be so kind as to let me know your decision.

About seven hundred prisoners were housed at the Alton prison, many of whom Thompson knew personally. Morale was very low among the men, but according to Thompson's memoirs, his arrival brought a surge of new hope for improved conditions or even escape. He brought them the latest war news and listened to their improbable escape plans while he began to devise a plan of his own. However, by the time he had finalized his plan to take over the prison, the administration, becoming fearful of an attack on the guard, transferred him briefly back to Gratiot Street Prison.

In September he was sent to the military prison on Johnson's Island in Lake Erie, near Sandusky, Ohio, where twenty-five hundred Confederates were being held. Although in summer, with its cooling breezes, the camp was quite endurable, what prisoners would most remember about Johnson's Island was the intense cold in winter. One inmate wrote that he was now convinced that "Hell has torments of cold." Others compared it to St. Helena and the Black Hole of Calcutta. The prisoners suffered in temperatures of 25 degrees below zero. Moreover, they were often hungry—so hungry that to supplement their meager rations, they were reduced to stalking, stewing, and eating rats. Rules for prisoners were posted, and a notice invited any prisoner to take an oath of allegiance to the United States and gain his freedom. In spite of the harsh conditions, few prisoners took advantage of the opportunity.

With his usual optimism, Thompson soon made himself at home in his new quarters and quickly assumed a leadership role among the prisoners. He first set about developing a directory of prisoners in the camp by asking each man to provide vital information about himself, such as where he was born, his rank, and where he was captured. When the directory was finished, the men were able to glean information from it about friends and relatives. The directory was useful to the prison administration as well, who could now better respond to inquiries about prisoners held on Johnson's Island or who had died there. Thompson also struck a deal with the administration whereby the men could write longer letters home than the one-page letter they had previously been allowed by paying two and a half cents for each additional page.

His next project was to improve the prison cemetery, which lay about half a mile outside camp. He and a group of volunteers measured the area, staked out rows of grave sites, and developed a map locating the graves of those already buried. Finally, he set himself up as a volunteer sexton of the cemetery to make sure that graves were dug properly, burials were recorded, and grave markers were repaired or replaced as needed.

Not surprisingly, Thompson soon earned the respect and admiration of both his captors and his fellow prisoners. While he was in the camp, he participated in a prisoner Thespian society and wrote poems for use in its performances. He began work on his memoirs. He seldom complained, and usually, any complaints or requests he did lodge were not for himself but for one or more of the other prisoners.

Sometimes Thompson was rewarded by indications that he had not been forgotten by his friends outside of prison, and he was always quick to express his appreciation for their support, as demonstrated by a letter he wrote Lieutenant Colonel William F. Pierson, U.S.A.:

> Your note of yesterday informing me that an unknown friend had left you fifty dollars for my use was received a few moments ago. You will please convey to this kind friend my sincere thanks and assure him that no human being shall ever need help if I have it in my power to assist him, and certainly no brave soldier though he may be my country's enemy, shall ever want where I . . . have the ability to provide for him.

Escape, however, was never far from Jeff Thompson's mind. His "grand plan" was to capture the garrison, then seize a ferry boat and capture Sandusky before taking off for Canada. He organized his men and set a date, which was delayed several times, until finally a gunboat that patrolled the lake came into the harbor and anchored between Johnson's Island and Sandusky. This effectively scuttled the escape plan.

Then winter began in earnest. Thompson wrote in his memoirs of having to "shiver and shake" in below-zero weather, despite wrapping himself in blankets. But he was quick to remind himself how much harder the intense cold must be for those who came from farther South, many of whom had never even seen snow. He wrote in his memoirs, "If I who had slept in the snows of the Rocky Mountains and the plains of Kansas and Nebraska through several winters had to shiver and shake—how much more these gentlemen from the sugar and cane fields among the orange groves and magnolias of the South must have suffered."

During Thompson's months in prison, the bloody guerrilla war in Missouri raged on. Guerrillas used various methods to terrorize their victims. Michael Fellman tells of one incident involving James Hamilton, "a well-known murdering guerrilla of southeastern Missouri," who stole into the home of Francis Tabor and intimidated his wife by suggesting that it was "easy to draw a knife across her husband's throat." Frequently guerrillas would "string up" a man to scare him into telling where he had hidden his money, or they would actually hang him. Once a gang of men, which included Frank and Jesse James, lured a farmer out of his house by saying they had lost their way and wanted his help. When he came out into the yard, they shot him five times and moved on.

Two of the most infamous Confederate guerrilla leaders were William Quantrill, a former teacher, and "Bloody Bill" Anderson, a wild and brutal raider. Upon joining Quantrill's organization, a new guerrilla would be asked only one question: "Will you follow orders, be true to your comrades, and kill those who serve and support the Union?"

On August 21, 1863, in the most notorious guerrilla attack of the war, Quantrill and nearly five hundred of his followers set out to raid the town of Lawrence, Kansas. Their intent was to destroy the town and kill all the men and boys. They ransacked

William Clarke Quantrill, a native of Ohio and a former schoolteacher, led his guerrilla band and others on the August 1863 raid on Lawrence, Kansas. He later had trouble controlling his men, and his biographer reports that in 1864 he was deposed at gunpoint by George Todd and left the band. Supposedly on his way to Virginia to fight with General Lee, he was shot in Kentucky by a Union guerrilla sent to kill him and died June 6, 1865. He was twenty-seven. *State Historical Society of Missouri, Columbia.*

and robbed homes, terrorized the homeowners, and torched their houses. When they completed their wild rampage, after killing at least 150 unarmed civilian men and boys and burning most of the town, the guerrillas raced back to Missouri, throwing away most of their loot on the way to lighten their load.

The border areas of Kansas and Missouri had a history of mutual distrust and animosity dating from the 1850s. Kansans resented the invasions of Missouri's "Border Ruffians" just as much as Missourians hated the incursions of Kansas "Jay-hawkers" and "Red Legs," so-called because of the red leggings they wore. The coming of the Civil War only inflamed this mutual enmity. Kansas Jayhawkers and Red Legs made raids into Missouri, plundering, killing, and burning farmhouses, and freeing hundreds of slaves. In return, Missouri bushwhack-ers sacked Kansas border settlements and shot down unarmed citizens.

Union officers along the border had decided that the only way to destroy the guerrilla movement was to strike at the root

Union General Thomas Ewing's Order Number 11 so outraged artist
George Bingham, who had remained a Union supporter, that he vowed
to make the general's action a symbol of the cruelties of war. He carried
out the threat, distributing etchings of his painting throughout Missouri.
State Historical Society of Missouri, Columbia.

of their power—the support they received from the civilian
population in Missouri. Following the Lawrence raid, enraged
Unionists of both Kansas and Missouri demanded that the
bushwhackers be crushed once and for all. Brigadier General
Thomas Ewing, then commander of the District of the Border,
agreed that strong action was needed and issued Order Number
11, the most drastic and repressive action directed against
civilians by the Union Army during the entire Civil War. This
order required that all residents of Jackson, Cass, Bates, and
northern Vernon Counties in Missouri who lived more than one
mile from specified military posts vacate their homes by
September 9. Approximately twenty thousand people were
forced to evacuate their homes, most of which were then
burned by Kansas troops.

Immediately, a huge outcry arose as large numbers of Missourians, both pro-Southern and Conservative Unionists, condemned the order. One of the most outspoken critics was the famous painter George Caleb Bingham, then serving as state treasurer. He went to see General Ewing and demanded that the order be rescinded. When Ewing refused, Bingham warned him that if the order was executed, he would make Ewing infamous with both pen and brush. Bingham kept his word. After his term as treasurer ended, he produced a painting titled *Martial Law* or *Order No. 11,* which depicts Ewing sitting on his horse watching his troops drive a Missouri family from its home. In the painting, a Kansas Red Leg is about to shoot an elderly family member despite the pleas of a beautiful young woman kneeling at his feet. The house is being pillaged by Union soldiers and, in the background, columns of smoke rise from burning fields. This painting did much to create the popular conception of General Ewing's Order Number 11.

Bingham also expressed his views in writing. He maintained that the order was an "act of purely arbitrary power," that it violated "every principle of justice," and that it was inspired by vengeance. Although much of his criticism was exaggerated, he was on firm ground when he denounced the severity of the order and the hardship and suffering it caused. His most important condemnation was also well-founded—that Order Number 11 utterly failed to achieve its stated purpose: to destroy the guerrillas. In fact, even after the war ended, continued guerrilla activity gave Missouri the label of "bandit state" for a number of years.

Order Number 11 quickly earned an odious reputation in Missouri and beyond, and Union authorities were forced to stop trying to enforce it. Nevertheless, although it was in some ways an understandable reaction by Union forces trying to quell guerrilla activity, it will long be remembered as one of the harshest aspects of the Civil War in Missouri.

6

The Final War Years, 1864-1865

~

My dear wife waits my coming,
My children lisp my name,
Kind friends would bid me welcome to my dear home again,
My father's grave is on the hill my boys lie in the vale,
I love each rock and murmuring rill,
Each mountain, wood and dale.
I'll suffer hardships, toil and pain,
For a good time's sure to come,
I'll battle long that I may gain my freedom and my home
I will return though foes may stand, disputing every rod;
My own dear home, my native land,
I'll win you—by God!

— M. Jeff Thompson, "Home, Sweet Home," M. J. Thompson Papers, Manuscripts Collection 72, Manuscripts Department, Howard Tilton Memorial Library, Tulane University, New Orleans

As 1864 began, Thompson and his fellow inmates on Johnson's Island continued to suffer from the intense cold. On January 1 it was 27 degrees below zero. Moreover, although they were surrounded by a lake, they also suffered from a shortage of drinking water. The cold weather froze the pumps, and the guards were afraid to let more than a few men at a time go from the fort to the shore to get buckets of water. Despite this precaution, however, the prisoners mounted a number of escape attempts. Some men tried bribing the guards while others dug tunnels. When the lake froze all the way to shore, two Union Army brigades were assigned to the area to serve as additional guards. As a result of this extra security measure, the prisoners were given greater freedom.

The men desperately needed some kind of recreation during the bleak winter days, so they organized an elaborate snowball war, with Thompson commanding one "army" of five hundred men and Colonel G. Troup Maxwell leading the opposing team. The engagement began on January 21 and lasted for three days. It included exchanges of prisoners, courts-martial, and humorous "official" reports and correspondence. Of course, numerous injuries resulted—noses were bloodied, teeth were knocked out, and men were buried in the snow. Unfortunately, a number of prisoners even died from their injuries or from exposure. Despite these tragedies, the snow battle provided the men a much-needed break from boredom as well as vigorous exercise. It gave them something to talk about during the dreary days of imprisonment.

In February, rumors of an upcoming prisoner exchange began to circulate throughout the camp, and eventually Thompson learned that he was among the three hundred men selected for the exchange. Guards took the prisoners to Sandusky, Ohio, then on to Point Lookout, Maryland, a large prison established in August 1863. But after a few days at Point Lookout, Thompson learned that instead of being exchanged, he would be going to Fort Delaware Military Prison, on the Delaware River below Wilmington. When the transfer was completed, Jeff was delighted to find that his new quarters at this island prison were the most comfortable he had yet experienced. He had a cheery room and a fellow prisoner as an orderly. In an effort to improve the lot of the other prisoners, he wrote various old friends in Philadelphia, Baltimore, New York, and Boston, asking for donations of warm clothing for the men. They responded by sending not only hundreds of suits of clothing but also other "comforts and favors" to the prisoners. Thompson said in his memoirs that, as a result, "we lived as sumptuously as I ever did in my whole life."

Basil Duke, a fellow prisoner at Fort Delaware, later wrote in his book *History of Morgan's Cavalry*, "General Thompson's military career is well known to his countrymen, but only his prison companions know how kind and manly he can be, under circumstances which severely try the temper. His unfailing flow of spirits kept everyone else in his vicinity cheerful, and his hopefulness was contagious." Moreover, Basil declared, "He possessed, also, an amazing poetical genius . . . Shut him up in a room with plenty of stationery, and in twenty-four hours, he would write himself up to the chin in verse." Apparently, Thompson intended to have his poetry published in a book after the war, but this was not to be.

While he was at Fort Delaware, one of the chaplains told Thompson that some ladies had asked what they could send him. Jeff responded that what he really needed was a pillow because he was using his coat as a substitute. The very next day, one of the women sent him a feather pillow, and he expressed his thanks by writing her a poem. The last stanza must have been particularly moving in its vision of an end to the miseries of war:

> I'll dream all night of pleasant scenes
> And home, with all its charms;
> My babes will greet me with their smiles,
> My dear wife with her arms.

Within a few days, every one of the men had received a pillow! Moreover, Thompson wrote in his memoirs that "if it had not been 'contraband of war' I would have had a feather bed."

About four months after his arrival at Fort Delaware, Thompson became one of the prisoners chosen to be used as "sacrifices" in a power struggle between the Union and Confederate forces. Sometime earlier, when Charleston, South

Carolina, was under siege by Union soldiers, Confederate Major General Samuel Jones had sent Union Major General John G. Foster a grim warning. In an effort to discourage enemy fire, he intended to confine fifty Union captives in sections of the city being bombarded by Union forces. To retaliate, the U.S. secretary of war promptly ordered fifty Confederate prisoners of equivalent rank to be exposed to Rebel shelling of his ships.

Thompson accepted this assignment with his usual cheerfulness. Although he did send his important personal papers home to St. Joseph for safekeeping, he declared, "a man's chance to be struck by lightning was better than to be hit by a siege gun." Actually, he seemed to be more apprehensive of suffering from seasickness than of being shot, and with good reason. Basil Duke recalled that "such stomach and lost dinners . . . came near taking the poetry out of General Thompson."

On June 24 he and the rest of the "target" group boarded a small steamboat and headed down the Delaware. After a three-day run, they arrived at Hilton Head, South Carolina, and were transferred to the brig *Dragoon*. To Thompson's dismay, he and the other prisoners on the ship were allowed on deck only a few hours each day. The rest of the time they were confined in the cramped quarters below deck where the temperature registered up to 130 degrees. This was a big change from the conditions at Fort Delaware!

Fortunately, before long word came that Confederate General Sam Jones was treating his Federal prisoners with consideration, and General Foster responded by allowing Thompson and the other prisoners to come on deck and amuse themselves with cards, chess, fishing, storytelling, and other such activities.

Jeff wrote numerous poems while he was incarcerated, many humorous, and in honor of this new assignment, he wrote one that began:

> If I had Sam Jones—I'd bruise his bones,
> Until I'm sure he'd tire,
> Of playing pranks, with captive Yanks,

> By placing them under fire.
> For here are we, brought down by sea,
> To try retaliation,
> And cuss the trick, I was made sea sick
> To appease the Yankee nation.

On his original handwritten copy of the poem, now in the M. Jeff Thompson Collection at Tulane University in New Orleans, Thompson noted,

> Written on the prison ship *Dragoon* at Hilton Head while one of the fifty who were sent down to be placed under fire in retaliation for fifty Federal officers who were placed in Charleston by Sam Jones of the Confederate Army. We were moored 'longside of the Frigate Wabash and guarded in the most vigilant manner—we suffered intensely from heat, and I would gladly have taken the danger of Big Guns in exchange for our situation on the prison ship.

Thompson wrote to his daughter from the *Dragoon*, "We are on a prison ship, and are having a pretty hard time, but my health is fine, and my spirits as cheerful as usual . . . You need not be uneasy, for I am not in the danger I will be after I am exchanged."

Late in July rumors again surfaced that prisoners were to be exchanged. Jeff scoffed at the news and declared that he would not believe it until he was free "in some swamp up to my waist in the water." But this time the rumors were true. On August 3, 1864, the long-hoped-for prisoner exchange took place. Even as they were pulling into Charleston harbor, Thompson sat moodily by himself, saying, "I don't believe a damned word of it. They will send us back on some red-tapeism yet." When Thompson was asked to make a speech by well-wishers who came down to the water's edge to greet the men, he said that for once he was not prepared but, as he wrote later, "I blurted out something that was anything but a speech."

Thompson had been in captivity nearly twelve months and

had spent time in six military prisons. He summarized his experience by remarking:

> I had been very cold and very hot, and very hungry and very thirsty, but neither did I suffer as much as I have when in the field with my command . . . consequently I retained my cheerfulness, never insulted my guards, and received every favor it was in their power to give me.

Upon their release, the men were given three months' pay and granted a thirty-day furlough. Thompson went to Richmond, and while he was there he visited with family members and old friends who still lived in the area. According to biographers, it was here that he learned the sad news that his wife had suffered another mental breakdown and would have to be confined to an asylum. In a poignant letter dated August 20, 1864, Emma wrote her husband about her confinement, saying, "I was not insane, darling, but oh—I had a congestive spell and it went to my head a little. They never sent for a doctor but took me to that asylum where I came near dying from fright and unkindness."

Thompson received orders to proceed to the Trans-Mississippi Department at Little Rock, which was now cut off from the rest of the Confederacy. Going by way of Atlanta, he was reunited with many of the men from his old command in St. Joseph.

Then he gradually made his way back to southeast Missouri to join up with General Sterling Price's "Army of Missouri." Price's trail in Missouri was easy to follow because by some accounts, including Thompson's, it was not unlike the destruction that Union General William T. Sherman left in his march across Georgia. In an earlier foray into Missouri from Arkansas, forces under the command of John S. Marmaduke had been accused of "wanton pillaging." Although Marmaduke denied the charges, Confederate officers had decided to deprive him of two of his four brigades. The pillaging continued during Price's raid, despite the efforts of some officers to stop it.

General Sterling Price had hoped throughout the war years to take Missouri, which he had served as governor from 1853 to 1857, for the Confederacy. Middle-aged when the war began, he was in poor health when he finally got his opportunity to take his Army of Missouri into the state and spent much of his time in his carriage. *State Historical Society of Missouri, Columbia.*

Pilot Knob, Missouri. After the Battle at Pilot Knob, Price decided not to carry out the planned attack on St. Louis but instead turned west. Thompson caught up with him near Potosi. *State Historical Society of Missouri, Columbia.*

General Thomas Ewing, a
Kansan, whose Order
Number 11 had outraged
Missourians, was commander
at Pilot Knob when Price
decided to attack the Union
garrison there. *State Historical
Society of Missouri, Columbia.*

Price's plan had been to move against St. Louis. He learned,
however, that the commander there, General William Rosecrans,
was calling together Union troops scattered in small groups
throughout Missouri. Eight thousand troops were encamped
south of the city. Also worrisome was a fifteen-hundred-man
infantry garrison at Pilot Knob, near Ironton, commanded by
General Thomas Ewing, which would be at his rear as he
advanced. Price had lost many of his Missourians to Rosecrans
at Corinth, Mississippi, two years earlier, and he consulted his
division commanders as to what to do. Jo Shelby wanted to continue to St. Louis, believing the infantry at Pilot Knob would not
be a danger, but Marmaduke and James Fagan advised him to
take Pilot Knob first.

Ewing, a Kansan, was generally hated throughout Missouri
and the Confederate States for his Order Number 11. He did not
want to be captured by Sterling Price's Army of Missouri, and
after Price's first assaults failed, resulting in heavy Confederate
losses, Ewing evacuated the fort during the night. Although

Shelby and Marmaduke chased him, he eventually made good his escape. In view of the heavy casualties he had suffered, Price decided to move west toward Jefferson City rather than proceed to St. Louis.

Price's army lived on whatever supplies it could gather as it marched, and Price himself was ill for a good part of the time. Eyewitness accounts of the "Rebel Raid" reveal an army in disarray. An interview with Etienne Toussin by special correspondent Dorothy O. Moore, published in the January 1, 1949, *St. Louis Globe Democrat*, illustrates the hardship the army caused one family. Toussin, a ninety-two-year-old fiddler, recalled, "General Sterling Price's Confederates swarmed all over Richwoods . . . General Price rode in the first plush-upholstered coach I had ever seen, drawn by a steel-gray team with all silver-trimmed harness." When Etienne got home he found:

> General Price was ill and had appropriated the canopied four-poster bed in our best guest room. Mother and the house slaves flew about waiting upon him, under orders, and his men were helping themselves to food. . . . They stayed three days and nights. Father, who was a Union sympathizer, although he had barracks of slaves, hid in a tree and watched them pillage the place. Mother sneaked food to him at night, and he slept on the ground. He caught cold and died later of tuberculosis. . . . Those soldiers slaughtered our cattle, hogs, took all our horses except a wild mare that eluded them in the woods. They drained the molasses barrel, took two barrels of pickles, kraut, hominy, dried beans, and coffee and emptied our root pit of carrots, potatoes, and cabbage. When they left we only had the mare, a crippled mule they had abandoned, and our appetites.

In his account of Price's raid, Gert Goebel of Franklin County described the destruction that took place in the communities along the Missouri River that had been settled by German immigrants in the decades before the war. But first at Union, some "Rebels from the area, who had gone South when the rebellion began, returned with this so-called army and avenged injustices their families supposedly suffered during their absence by the murders of several Unionists who were suspected of sharing the guilt. . . . the thirst for vengeance was in general the main cause of the murders during the raid."

The army separated at Union. Price and Shelby moved toward Jefferson City, "with the pack of thieves which accompanied the army spread out over several miles to the right and left of the main corps, robbing and plundering."

Marmaduke led a vanguard toward Hermann, a known Union town, to get badly needed supplies and horses. Washington, in Franklin County, had been evacuated, and there men went into stores and helped themselves to clothes and whatever else they needed or wanted. Moving west, what they needed most was horses, "for theirs had for the most part been so exhausted by hard riding and so starved that they were literally nothing but skin and bones."

Reaching Hermann, they were met by unexpected gunfire, tricking them at first into believing they were facing Union forces. When the firing stopped, Marmaduke's men finally discovered an old cannon that several older men had dragged from hill to hill, firing from each hill to give the impression that the Confederates were facing a Union force. The angry Confederates threw the cannon into the river and proceeded to take everything they could ride and carry as they moved west to meet Price at Jefferson City.

At first Thompson, who caught up with Price near Potosi, accompanied the expedition as an officer without command, which must have seemed strange to him. But on October 6 when Colonel David Shanks, the commanding officer of one of General Jo Shelby's brigades, was mortally wounded near Jefferson City, Price placed Thompson in command of Shanks's brigade. This "Iron Brigade," formerly commanded by Shelby himself, was considered by historian Albert Castel to be "by far the best fighting brigade" in Price's army. "It was made up of veteran, battle-hardened Missourians, each of which carried several revolvers

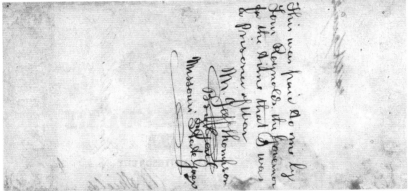

Thompson wrote on the back of this bill, "This was paid to me by Tom Reynolds, the Governor for the time that I was a a prisonor of war." He signed it "M. Jeff Thompson, Brig. Genl Missouri State Guard." *University of Missouri Western Historical Manuscript Collection, Columbia.*

in addition to a carbine or rifle." Unlike their new commander, they "had long since discarded the sabre as worthless."

Among the politicians accompanying the army was Governor-in-exile Thomas Reynolds. Remembering Thompson from the early days of the war, Reynolds gave him the pay due him for the months he had spent in prison. Reynolds carried the State Seal, taken from Jefferson City as Jackson's government had fled in 1861, and he had hoped to reclaim the capital. Price camped about two miles south of Jefferson City

Born in Randolph County, Missouri, William "Bloody Bill" Anderson became the most notorious guerrilla on either side of the war, according to Charles Mink. Shortly before his meeting with General Sterling Price, he had led a raid on Centralia, terrorizing the inhabitants, robbing the stage that arrived, and massacring unarmed Union soldiers on a north Missouri train. He was killed in Ray County on October 24, 1864, with Price's orders in his pocket. *State Historical Society of Missouri, Columbia.*

where, according to legend, he slept in another four-poster bed at the home of the Wallendorf family. Dino Brugioni, conducting research for *The Civil War in Missouri as Seen from the Capital City,* found a photograph of the bed and reported that Price paid the family twenty-seven dollars in Confederate currency for his room and board, but according to legend his men killed all the livestock except one chicken that escaped to the woods and took all Wallendorf's horses, leaving their own in exchange.

Much to Reynolds's dismay, Price, seeing the Union fortifications around the city, ordered his army to continue toward Boonville. There he met with Bill Anderson and George Todd, who had taken over the Quantrill men As Richard S. Brownlee wrote, considering his situation, Price had determined to use these guerrillas, or "partisans," as he called them. He reported later:

Captain Anderson, who reported to me that day with a company of almost 100 men was immediately sent to destroy the North Missouri Railroad. At the same time, Quantrill was sent with the men under his command to destroy the Hannibal and Saint Joseph Railroad, to prevent the enemy, if possible, from throwing their forces to my front from St. Louis. These officers, I was informed, did effect some damage to the roads, but none of any material damage, and totally failed in the main object proposed, which was to destroy the large railroad bridge that was in the end of Saint Charles County.

According to Brownlee, George Todd and his newly acquired gang were sent to destroy the Pacific Railroad, a task in which they succeeded by "burning the bridge, depot, water tanks, and houses in Otterville in Cooper County." But, he reported, "Neither Anderson nor Quantrill paid much attention" to Price's orders. Some historians believe Quantrill, who had been camped out in southern Howard County most of the summer, never received Price's order, but he and Anderson were both in Glasgow when Shelby captured the town and both took the opportunity to rob private citizens. Anderson followed Price's army west and Quantrill left the area for the East later in the year.

Under Thompson's command, the "Iron Brigade" performed well. On October 10, with Price camped in Saline County, Jeff Thompson took twelve hundred of Shelby's Confederate cavalrymen to raid Sedalia. He had intended to continue to a German settlement in Lafayette County that had often been raided by guerrillas, but hearing there were Federal troops in the area, he rode northward instead and joined Price the next day east of Grand Pass.

Thompson was much disturbed by the amount of plundering by the officers and men at Boonville. He wrote in his memoirs, "Many officers and men loaded themselves, their horses and wagons with 'their rights.'" When the capture of Sedalia was accomplished, he ordered his men to line up and remain in line while he directed the quartermasters, commissaries, and ordnance officers to requisition what was needed. At first, the officers had difficulty controlling their men until Thompson "spanked" a few looters with his sabre and reportedly shot a mule from under one would-be robber. As a result, Thompson could later claim with satisfaction, "To my personal knowledge, not one man appropriated a single article to his private use."

Price, remembering the men who had followed him after Wilson's Creek and Lexington in 1861, had expected that when he entered Missouri his army would attract large numbers of volunteers and find widespread support among the citizenry. He was disappointed. The Civil War in Missouri had been anything but civil. When General Sherman made his famous declaration years after the war, "War is hell, boys," he may not have had Missouri in mind, but it aptly described life for many Missourians.

In August 1861, John C. Fremont had issued an emancipation proclamation freeing the slaves of all who resisted the Federal government and declaring Missouri to be in a state of martial law. Lincoln rescinded Fremont's emancipation proclamation and soon relieved him of duty, but the state remained under martial law. For three years the Union military command superceded the existing civil government. That action led to a number of tyrannical acts against the state's citizens, which ranged from arbitrary arrest and imprisonment to murder of prisoners, from illegally taking nonessential supplies to outright robbery, pillage, and arson. Anyone could be arrested and detained for an indefinite period on mere suspicion of disloyalty because martial law provided for the suspension of habeas corpus, the normal rule of law under which anyone who is arrested must be informed of the charges against him or be released within a short time. As a result, the U.S. Army arrested more civilians in Missouri than in any other state.

While these excesses of martial law and abuses by the military government during the war did not actually give birth to guerrilla warfare, they greatly intensified what Michael Fellman, in his book *Inside War: The Guerrilla Conflict in Missouri during the American Civil War,* called "the most widespread, longest-lived and most destructive guerrilla war in the Civil War." Bands on both sides of the conflict roamed the state, taking revenge on supporters of the other. Unfortunately, as Richard Brownlee commented in *Gray Ghosts of the Confederacy,* Missouri's state militia proved as insubordinate and lawless as the troops from Kansas "raiding across the border." According to Gert Goebel, in some of the western "old slave counties" in which the "Rebel element" predominated, "militia units were formed that consisted entirely of Rebels." In these so-called Paw-Paw Militia units, those counting on the Confederacy to win enjoyed the comforts of home while doing their part for the South by preying on their neighbors "rather than suffering the dangers, hardships, and privations of the regular Southern army."

Though disappointed that the lack of response to his call for volunteers forced him to rely on guerrillas, General Price pushed on into the west-central portion of Missouri, and at Westport in Jackson County he engaged the Union force in a three-day battle—later called the Gettysburg of the West. Shelby's brigade was given the task of leading the advance, but he later frankly admitted that in the face of a massive counterattack, there was nothing to do "but to run for it." In the end Price was defeated, Marmaduke was captured, and Shelby and Thompson had the duty of covering the retreat. Camped across the river from Jefferson City with Price's army, Marmaduke, whose father had been elected lieutenant governor in 1840 and served briefly as governor after the suicide of Governor Thomas Reynolds, had reportedly pointed to the capitol building and told his men he would come back some day as governor. Ironically, his boast was realized. Promoted to major general while in prison in Massachusetts, he eventually returned to Missouri, where he was elected governor in 1884. He died in office in 1887.

After the Westport defeat, Price's "Army of Missouri" retreated through Kansas, southern Missouri, Arkansas, and the Indian Territory, finally entering Texas. Although Thompson still

John Sappington Marmaduke, born near Arrow Rock in Saline County, was captured after the Battle of Westport. He later became governor of Missouri. *State Historical Society of Missouri, Columbia.*

held only his state brigadier's commission, he sometimes had charge of an entire division. By the time he and his men reached Texas, they had fought in a number of skirmishes and battles including the Battle of Newtonia and the Battle of Mine Creek. In his book *General Sterling Price and the Civil War in the West,* Castel declared, "Wilson's Creek was the first great battle of the war west of the Mississippi, and Mine Creek the last." Castel praised Thompson's report of the battle as "a more sober and no doubt more accurate account of Shelby's rear guard action" than Shelby himself gave.

The men were suffering from being constantly on the move with too little food, too little sleep, and too little clothing for the cold rain, sleet, and snow through which they trudged. On foot along with his men, Thompson had it even worse because he was still making do with the summer clothing he had worn on the prison ship at Charleston. But it was not in his nature to complain, and at year's end he wrote in his memoirs only, "Thus ended the year 1864, of which I had spent seven months in prison and five months in the saddle."

Early in 1865, Thompson was finally able to obtain a new tailor-made uniform, the style of which made him look even taller than he was. As he commented wryly, "I look tall enough for a lightning rod." He received orders from General Kirby Smith to take command of the northern sub-district of Arkansas, which included northern Arkansas and much of Missouri. By this time the troops were a pretty ragtag group. They suffered from low morale and seemed to be more interested in plundering than in fighting a war. Moreover, numerous guerrilla bands and other outlaw groups had infested the area. In his determination to restore discipline among the troops and drive out the criminal element, Thompson asked for and was given dictatorial powers, including the power of life and death, over not only his men but also any outlaws he might capture. With a staff of ten men, Jeff set out on his next mission, traveling across rivers, flooded areas, and swamps to reach Harrisburg, Arkansas. On March 20 he assumed command of the district and set up his headquarters. One of his first actions was to outlaw all guerrillas.

Then came the beginning of the end. On April 18, just nine days after the surrender of General Robert E. Lee and four days after President Lincoln was mortally wounded by an assassin's bullet, Thompson received a flag of truce from Union Major General J. J. Edwards demanding his surrender. But General Jeff Thompson was not yet ready to give up. He "respectfully and most positively" declined to surrender because he still believed in the ultimate victory of the Confederate cause and was determined to fight to the end. He redoubled his efforts to inject some enthusiasm into his command—but with little or no success. He engaged in some delaying tactics, trying to postpone the inevitable. He was especially opposed to surrendering on May 10, the anniversary of the first blood shed in Missouri following the capture of Camp Jackson, where Lyon's volunteers had fired on bystanders as they marched the captured state militia to the U.S. arsenal.

Finally, however, Thompson was forced to concede defeat.

When he learned that President Davis had been captured, he said, "I bowed my head to the blow with all the resignation in my nature and advised all to submit with the best grace possible." He realized that if he did not surrender, the Union army would carry out its threat to devastate the entire area and treat his soldiers as outlaws. Besides, he could gather together only a few of his scattered troops.

Even in surrender, General Thompson maintained his sense of drama. Because the men under his command were scattered over such a wide area, he insisted it would be necessary to hold two surrender ceremonies at different locations, one on May 25 at Wittsburg on the St. Francis River and the other on June 5 at Jacksonport where the Black and White Rivers joined. He wanted to bring his men himself, and he received the same surrender terms as those given to General Lee.

In the book *Old Man River: The Memories of Captain Louis Rosche,* by Robert A. Hereford, Rosche tells how excited he was when his boat, the *Arkansas,* was chartered by the government to parole Thompson and his army. Paroling meant that the surrendering troops would take an oath of allegiance to the United States and give up their arms, after which they were free to return to their homes. When the boat docked at Wittsburg Landing, the Swamp Fox was waiting, seated on a white horse, surrounded by his sorry-looking band of men. Some of them were riding horses as hungry-looking as themselves. Most were ragged, and some were even without shoes.

Thompson led the way, walking his white horse up the gangplank, dismounting, and going to the table, where he signed the waiting document. Next, 193 officers marched aboard and were paroled. Then it was time for the soldiers to step up, stack their guns, and sign their paroles. The first Rebel walked to the table, then strode to the rail and tossed his gun into the river.

A Union officer stepped forward angrily, his hand reaching for his sword, but Colonel Davis stopped him with a sharp command. The rest of the men advanced and signed but, according to Rosche, the proceedings were punctuated by the sound of

Following the Battle of Westport, Price's army retreated south to Texas. *Reprinted by permission of Louisiana State University Press, from Richard S. Brownlee,* Gray Ghosts of the Confederacy: Guerrilla Warfare in the West, 1861–1865. *Copyright 1958, Louisiana State University Press.*

guns striking the water. At the end, only a few broken guns were stacked on the deck.

The process of paroling took two days for the first group. At tables where the muster rolls had been set up, each man signed or made his mark, his name was recorded, and his oath of allegiance accepted. Then the men received their rations, which Thompson had demanded—hardtack, bacon, sugar, coffee, and rice, among other items. As Thompson described it,

> One pocket would be filled with salt, another with sugar, another with coffee, the hat with hard bread. They drank the vinegar, put a bar of soap under one arm and the bacon under the other, [holding] the candles, rice, dried apples, etc. as best they could in their hands.

On June 5, 1865, he dramatically surrendered his final group of 111 officers and 4,854 enlisted men. In an impassioned farewell speech to his troops, he told the men to go home, obey the law, and cooperate with authorities. He railed against those in his command whose behavior had been less than honorable. In part of his speech, he said, "I now come to surrender you and hope you will make better citizens than you have soldiers . . . I know there are some gentlemen here, and I know there are some damned, sneaky, cowardly dogs who have never done nothing on nary side."

When someone in the crowd shouted, "Talk to us like gentlemen, Sir!" the general shouted, "ATTENTION!" When their military training made them pause, Thompson continued, "If you men don't stand and listen to me, there are enough one-leg and one-arm men and sick soldiers with honorable discharges in their pockets among you to whip all the balance, and I'll tell them to do it."

In *Missouri Yesterdays,* Louise Platt Hauck of St. Joseph wrote that the June 5, 1865, speech caused much bitterness among his Southern supporters, "but he explained that during his years in prison his command had scattered and the original troops replaced by 'the rougher element . . . on the outskirts of every army.'" Many, he pointed out to them, had been "skulking for the last three years in the swamps within a few miles" of their own homes.

When all the informalities and formalities of surrendering his men were finally over, Thompson boarded a steamship for Memphis. He took off his uniform and, in a typically dramatic gesture, presented the white plume on his hat to the ship's commanding officer. When he arrived at Memphis, he went to a bar and indulged in what he called "an old fashioned drink of bourbon whiskey, the first honest drink I had taken since 22 January, 1863." The war was over at last.

7

After the War

I am sitting here tonight, friend,
The last night of the year—
And am thinking of the gloomy past,
And all the friends so dear
Who have fallen in the horrid war
Which recently scourged our land;
And I mourn for them, the noble dead,
Of our chivalrous Southern band.

—M. Jeff Thompson, December 31, 1865,
M. Jeff Thompson Papers, Manuscripts Collection 72,
Manuscripts Department, Howard-Tilton Memorial
Library, Tulane University, New Orleans

After M. Jeff Thompson surrendered his men and received his parole, he never went back to St. Joseph to live. Many of his contemporaries found it so difficult to accept the fact that the South had lost the war that they fled the United States. Sterling Price and other Missouri Confederates, including Jo Shelby, left for Mexico rather than surrender. On the other hand, Thompson, ever the pragmatist, immediately began to adjust to a nation in which the North had won. He was one of the first Southern leaders to be "reconstructed," signing

St. Joseph historian Bartlett Boder reported in 1952 that when he visited the Confederate Museum in New Orleans, this portrait of M. Jeff Thompson, then in an ornate oval frame, was on display. The portrait is no longer on display, but a copy of the portrait remains in the museum's collection. *Courtesy of the Confederate Memorial Hall Museum, New Orleans. Claude Levet photographer.*

the oath of allegiance to the United States and serving as a model for others by speaking out in favor of Reconstruction, of rebuilding the South. On June 6, 1865, the day after his surrender, civilian Jeff Thompson wrote a letter to Major General G. M. Dodge, commander of the Department of Missouri, offering to provide information relative to his military service. "I have observed the laws of civilian warfare," he declared. "There is no man in the country where I have commanded that can, with truth, say that he has been punished by me for his political opinions, and certainly no enemy has found me otherwise than a fair and chivalrous soldier."

On the same day, he sent a letter to President Andrew Johnson asking to be reinstated as a citizen of the United States: "In conformity with the proviso in your Proclamation of May 20, 1865, I hereby apply for permission to take the Amnesty Oath, prescribed in said Proclamation, and to become again a citizen of the United States."

Thompson actually took the oath of allegiance a little later in New Orleans, although he never had an answer to his letter to the president. During the rest of his life, he worked diligently to end regional and sectional hostilities and to promote the economic and social redevelopment of the South, which he realized would require assistance from the North. He wrote letters to his Southern friends, asking them to accept the situation and work to reorganize under the laws of Congress. He was outspoken in his opposition to a few Southern politicians who tried to convince the South that the country would be ruined if they were excluded from holding office. He wrote many letters to newspaper editors. The *Louisville Journal,* in 1867, printed a long letter from Thompson in which he outlined his views on Reconstruction, saying, in part:

> I can simply set my soldiers an example of patience, industry, and enterprise to build up our broken fortunes and make the land bloom again in peace, confidence, and plenty. . . . Abstract ideas or obsolete theories shall not govern me, for I will look facts in the face as they exist, and make the best of the future, without moping over the past.

Thompson was also involved in numerous activities to help victims of the war. When the Ladies Benevolent Association of St. Joseph staged a fair in 1866 to raise funds for the war poor of the South, Thompson's sister, a member of the organization, asked him for a contribution. He had no money to give, but ever the wordsmith, Thompson penned a long poem in honor of the occasion, a copy of which is in the Thompson papers at the University of Missouri Western Historical Manuscript Collection in Columbia. He sent copies to his sister, and she collected funds by selling them. The poem, titled "An Appeal for the Widows and Orphans from the Confederates in Heaven," reads in part:

For years we marched, for months we stood beneath the
    battle smoke,
And hunger, cold, and sickness faint, would hearts less true
    have broke,
But cheerfully we bore it all; and went down, one by one,
Each hoping, as he gave his life, your freedom had been
    won.

And now we stand, a glorious host, in our home above the
    clouds,
And the ragged soldiers from the ditch have sunbeams for
    their shrouds;
Rough, bearded men, and fair haired boys, are clothed alike
    in beauty,
For all have died at honor's post; each one has done his
    duty.

The war had destroyed Thompson's economic resources, and he was never able to restart his business career. He first went to Memphis, where, in an attempt to return to civilian life, he opened a commission house where he sold groceries and liquor. This business failed, and he went next to New Orleans, where for two years he tried unsuccessfully to make a living as a merchant. An announcement printed March 1, 1866, and preserved in the Missouri Historical Society in St. Louis indicates that "M. Jeff Thompson, Late Brig. Gen. C.S.A." with "Richard Power, Late of Arkansas" and "Charles T. Perrie, Late of Missouri," were opening a business, M. Jeff Thompson and Co., at 50 Canal Street. The "Wholesale Grocers and Commission Merchants" promised to "Keep always on hand A Full Assortment of Plantation Supplies, Boat and Bar Stores." Despite a long, persuasive letter in verse from Thompson to prospective customers, the company apparently did not prosper.

Although his business ventures continued to fail, his ability to make friends still flourished. Albert L. Lee, a Union general and former St. Joseph banker now in the state of Louisiana's Reconstruction program, used his influence to have Thompson appointed chief engineer on the Levee Commission of the Board of Public Works of the State of Louisiana, with headquarters in New Orleans. Thompson held this position until shortly before his death. Because of this, he earned the contempt of some of his onetime Southern compatriots, who called him a traitor, but while in the position he designed an ambitious program for improving the swamps of Louisiana.

In a story entitled "M. J. Jeff Thompson," dated February 16, 1867, the *St. Joseph Vindicator* wrote:

> We had a call on Saturday from General M. J. Thompson who is domiciliated in New Orleans. He says he is astonished at the rapidity of the work of reconciliation that is going on in the South. He had no idea that things would wheel into line so quick and so soon after the subsidence of the storm. He says he is going to work, and everybody else that he knows of in the South seems to have a "realizing sense" of the necessity and desirableness of that very thing. The only persons who want more fighting are those who didn't do any when there was a chance to fight.

On November 29, 1872, Thompson formally relinquished his parental rights to his youngest daughter, Marcie, then twelve years old, so that his sister Betty and her husband—the only parents Marcie had ever known—could adopt her. In a poignant Transfer of Paternity document, he stated:

> I Jeff Thompson . . . in consideration of love for and confidence in John James Abell and Betty Thompson Abell his wife give bequeath and envest to and in them all my legal rights of possession and paternity to Martha Washington Thompson, my daughter who was born in the city of St. Joseph, Missouri on the 22nd day of February 1860. . . . As this document may become a matter of record the following facts should be stated. In the spring of 1861 when Martha was being weaned that physical fact combined with the religious fervor of Lent and the excitement of anticipated war

so affected Mrs. Thompson that she became deranged and had to be taken to an Asylum soon afterwards I came South to the war and John J. Abell and my sister Betty took charge of my children. During the war Mrs. Thompson recovered and took possession of our other children and with the exception of two visits to us in New Orleans [Martha] has grown up under the charge and care of her Aunt and Uncle and knows them with the confidence and affection of a daughter and desires to remain with them as such. . . . Mrs. Thompson has relapsed and is now in an Asylum.

Despite his personal tragedies, Thompson continued to draw attention to himself, and newspapers always found him to be good copy. One wrote of him:

Jeff Thompson, ex-rebel general, is now surveyor general of Louisiana and is thus described: long, gaunt, ugly, and garrulous, Jeff haunts the saloons and takes the oath of allegiance (with a little sugar) as often as his fellow citizens invite him. His stock remark is: "I change my religion every week, my politics every day, and my opinion every hour, and yet I can't keep up."

In a rebuttal story, another reporter wrote: "Ex-rebel? Well, what of that? Jeff Thompson was brave enough to fight for his principle he then advocated, and today he would do what many a politician would not do—he would fight for the party and State who have given him his present position of State Engineer."

As was his wont, he worked so hard that he soon destroyed his health, which had already been damaged by tuberculosis he had contracted in prison. Thompson left Louisiana in early July 1876, apparently hopeful that a long vacation and change of climate might improve his failing health. He went to New York and to the Centennial Exposition in Philadelphia, then traveled to St. Joseph to visit relatives and friends. While there, his condition worsened, and he died in his room at the Pacific House, owned by his brother-in-law John J. Abell, on September 5, 1876. He was fifty years old.

That his adopted city had not forgotten him was borne out by a statement in his obituary in the *St. Joseph Gazette:* "Jeff Thompson was a favorite with all who knew him . . . as an evidence of his popularity, we need only to mention the fact that a letter came yesterday, just about the hour of his death, soliciting him to make the opening address at the coming fair in Charleston."

Years later, in another *St. Joseph Gazette* article, dated April 1, 1919, Louise Platt Hauck wrote:

> The historical records of Missouri speak of him as one of the noted figures of the day. He was wined and dined by Davis, and at the close of the war was a guest of General Grant at his summer home. One of his contemporaries says of him, "You couldn't always approve of him, but you couldn't help admiring him."

8

The Man and His Legacy

My father's father was a rebel,
And Mother's father was a rebel too,
So when the South called out her soldiers
Pray what else would you have me do?
But buckle on my father's sabre,
And seize at once his trusty gun,
And strike a blow for Southern freedom,
Like old Virginia's faithful son?

—M. Jeff Thompson, Thompson memoirs

I f Jeff Thompson seems "larger than life" to us today, it may be, at least in part, because he deliberately helped to create his own image and legend. Certainly, his short life had many elements of the romantic Civil War hero—he was a descendant of Revolutionary War officers and distantly related to George Washington. He lost his mother at an early age. At seventeen he left home, and from then on, as he put it, he "paddled his own canoe." He made—and lost—a fortune in St. Joseph. Before the war, he was one of the most popular men in northwest Missouri. When the Civil War came, he left his family, a comfortable home, and an established place in the community to fight for a losing cause. Committed to what he considered fair and honorable

A mural by George Gray on display in the Pony Express National Museum in St. Joseph commemorates General M. Jeff Thompson's contribution to the city and some of his activities during the Civil War. *State Historical Society of Missouri, Columbia.*

behavior, Thompson was a man of great industry and accomplishments. Although he was without formal military training or a past record of military success, he nevertheless proved to be a master of the arts of warfare in the early years of the Civil War.

Bruce Catton, in his book *The Coming Fury*, described Thompson as "an energetic eccentric." Elmo Ingenthron, in *Borderland Rebellion: A History of the Civil War on the Missouri-Arkansas Border,* wrote that "the name Jeff Thompson was known in virtually every household, the object of either praise or belittlement, but always the object of curiosity." He was courageous, foolhardy, egotistical, and impulsive. He has also been called "a man of contradictions," an "erratic genius," and the "poet laureate of the marshes." After the war, he was frequently labeled a turncoat by fellow Southerners. He was admired and scorned, despised and beloved—but seldom ignored.

Although he has often been characterized as a shadowy Civil War character, Thompson led large numbers of men but was never commissioned in the Confederate army. His military exploits reflected both his courage and his foolhardiness. Louise Platt Hauck wrote that he was "brave to a point of recklessness, no mission was too desperate for him." A newspaper article, written while Thompson was at the Johnson's Island prison, stated, "Jeff Thompson, we must say, fights as bravely as he talks."

Chivalry, romance, and the far horizon always fascinated Thompson. He loved horses and was an excellent horseman, he was gallant to the ladies, and he wrote poetry to commemorate almost every important occasion. He was compassionate when he took prisoners, and he was often lauded for his courtesy to his captives. His memoirs sparkle with adventure. Jay Monaghan quoted Thompson's daughter Marcie as saying that the notes he left "read like a romance. Had it filled out the details, they would be a mine of information." Like Jeb Stuart, another colorful wartime hero of the Confederacy, Jeff Thompson was bold, dashing, and resourceful. Although he was a strict disciplinarian, he was popular with his men and fellow officers. He was the kind of man myths are made of. He took pride in living up to the tradition of his forebears. To him, victory wasn't the point—honor was. He was determined to be true to his lineage and to the tradition of American liberty.

It has been said that the story of any man's life can reveal attributes of the historical period in which he lived. This is certainly true of Jeff Thompson. A Southerner by birth, he chose to fight from the divided state of Missouri, his adopted home. He fought on the losing side of the war, often using the guerrilla-style tactics that were so prevalent in Missouri at the time. As soon as the war was over, he petitioned the U.S. government to reinstate his citizenship, boasted of being a houseguest of General Ulysses S. Grant, and spoke out regularly and vigorously in favor of reconciliation.

His appearance was often flamboyant. He sometimes rode a white horse and sported a white plume in his hat. He has been variously described by others as "nearly six feet tall and as slender as a pair of tongs," as "tall, sinewy, weather-beaten," and as "a queer looking genius dressed in a suit of snowy white from the plume in his hat to the heel of his boot, and with a sword belt and white gloves . . . full of fun . . . and an incessant talker." He was apparently not conventionally handsome—in fact, he claimed he was once awarded a pocketknife for being the ugliest man at a county fair. However, one reporter said of him that "his handsome deeds make amends for what he lacks in personal beauty."

Thompson described himself to be "full six feet" tall and weighing 135 pounds. On the other hand, St. Louis newspapers liked to say that he was only five feet eight inches tall and dressed in a very unmilitary costume.

When strangers met him, they usually responded warmly to his self-confident manner, his broad smile, and his forthrightness. They liked his friendly blue eyes and long blond hair, which he darkened with oil and tucked behind his ears. One newspaper said, "he has a smiling red face, a pleasant face indeed—and his manner is quite agreeable, although dashed with the leaven of his well-known egotism." His troops were always fascinated by the way he could pucker his face and close his jaws with a snap to emphasize a point he was making. While still a young man, he had lost so many of his teeth that he could flatten out his already long face and make it as chinless as a snake's head.

He loved to tell stories and often made himself the hero. One oft-repeated anecdote concerned the way in which he enforced his ban on horse-stealing among his troops. As Thompson told it, when one of his soldiers was caught with a stolen horse and brought to Thompson, the following conversation took place:

> "Did you steal the horse?"
> "Yes!"
> "Had you seen my order on the subject?"
> "Yes."

"Did you know that I would hang you if you were caught?"

"Well, I thought you might."

"Are you a married man?"

"Yes, but I do not live with my wife."

"Which party do you belong to?"

"I am a Southern man."

"Well, sir, I am glad to hear it, but nevertheless I will hang you at three o'clock this afternoon, so get ready."

"General, it is damned hard to hang a man for doing what everybody is doing."

"Yes, it is hard, but it is fair. The practice must be stopped, and somebody must be hung to stop it, and I might as well hang you as anybody else."

In due course the man was hanged, and Thompson ended the story by saying that after he and three more horse thieves were executed, the horse-stealing stopped.

Thompson often put his own spin on a story or report to put himself and/or his troops in the most favorable light—to minimize a defeat or embellish his successes. Often, but not always. On one occasion, after his troops had torn down the flag in the town of Commerce, Missouri, he rode up to a crowd of ladies to assure them of their safety. One of the women asked, "Are you General Thompson, sir?" When he said yes, she said, "I am Mrs. Eversole, sir . . . I want to know what you cut down that flag for, you cowardly rascal!" and she advanced, cracking her fists and adding, "If you will get off that horse, I will whip you right here." With a grin, he replied that he would "decline the honor" of being whipped by her, and he rode away.

Although he usually tried to appear strong and fearless, at times he let down his guard and admitted his own human weaknesses. Early in the war, he wrote in his memoirs that "the earnest anxiety which constantly preys upon my mind, and the weighty responsibility of leading an attack with my limited military knowledge, continually exhausted me." Still, there is no doubt that he was courageous. General Jo Shelby, after the battle of Newtonia, wrote in his report, "Brigadier General M. Jeff Thompson needs nothing here to establish a reputation already known over the United States. He was always with his brigade, and that was always where the fight was heaviest."

In another reflective moment, Thompson wrote, "I have read beautiful descriptions of battle fields . . . but with me, such things have always been stern reality, born of terrible necessity, and the poetry comes when a comfortable parlor and glass of hot whiskey punch lends the enchanted distance to the view."

He delighted in issuing proclamations, and a historian wrote of him in the 1890s:

> General M. Jeff Thompson was a man of ability, but it was not strictly of a military order. He excelled at using proclamations and manifestos. Every document of that sort, whether issued by a Federal officer, from the President of the United States to the colonel of a Home Guard regiment was sure to bring an answer in kind from him.

One of Thompson's proclamations, which received wide circulation, urged the people to

> Leave your plows in the furrow, your ox to the yoke, and rush like a tornado upon our invaders and foes to sweep them from the face of the earth, or force them from the soil of our state! . . . We have plenty of ammunition and the cattle on ten thousand hills are ours.

Newspapers that published this proclamation were quick to point out that Thompson's claim was for even more than the thousand claimed for God by the biblical writer of the Psalms. In addition to the amusement and sometimes scorn generated by this proclamation, it caused Thompson another small personal defeat, described by Walter Stevens in *Centennial History of Missouri: One Hundred Years in the Union 1820–1921*. Not long after the issue of Thompson's appeal, he sent a scouting party out for fresh meat. The scouts took the only cow of a poor widow. She rushed into the camp and accosted Thompson. "Why, General," she protested, "is it possible that you intend to rob a widow of the only cow she has in the world, when, as you have said in your proclamation, the cattle on ten thousand hills are yours?" The general grinned and ordered the cow returned to the widow.

Thompson delighted in the press coverage of his exploits and boasted, "Everyone gives me credit for having 7000 men, and I have frightened them to death." Of course, not all of the coverage was positive, especially in the Northern papers, which once reported Thompson to be "most of the time in a condition of drunkenness" and another time said he was "despised in Memphis."

Thompson would not tolerate dishonesty—either in himself or from those in his command. He fiercely criticized officers who permitted plundering and would not allow his men to take anything not essential to the welfare of the army.

He was quick to react to any remark that reflected on the honor of his family or friends, and he wrote numerous letters to the newspaper editors or other guilty individuals, challenging their truthfulness and taking them to task for what he termed slander.

When the Yazoo, Mississippi, *Banner* published an article criticizing certain former Confederate leaders, Jeff responded with contempt:

> From the style in which you speak, I judge you to have been one of those miserable, dirty dogs, who published an eight-by-ten sheet during the war for no earthly purpose but to avoid conscription, and who, to cover up their own cowardice, tried to . . . break down some of the purest and noblest men in the Confederacy.

Although the war disrupted Thompson's home life, as it did for thousands of others, he tried, whenever possible, to make provisions for his wife to visit him, sometimes accompanied by one or more of their children. Not only was he away from his family for long periods, leaving his wife and children to manage without him, but in addition, his wife, like many other Missouri women of the time, suffered many hardships and indignities. Reacting to an article in the *Chicago Journal,* which apparently contained statements he felt were uncomplimentary to his wife, he wrote a letter to the editor labeling the remarks slanderous and ended by saying, "You will please let me know the correspondent's name and address for in coming years . . . there will be many private accounts to settle with those who have been too officious and zealous, and I would be pleased to know this man, . . . that I may teach him better manners."

In response to another disparaging article that also mentioned his wife, he retorted, "This person's description of me is, as he would make me appear, amusing and ridiculous, but it is too bad that he should . . . speak so of a lady whose very tracks in the dust he would not be worthy to look upon."

Thompson was devoted to his children, and because he was away from home so much he made it a point to write them special letters on each birthday. In one such letter to his youngest daughter, Marcie, the one who had been the most deprived of her father's presence, he wrote assuring her of his love and his regrets at being so long separated from her and the rest of his family:

> You are four years old this day, and I will write to you, that, in future years, when you have grown up, and I (will) probably be in my grave, you can read this and know that I love you dearly though I have seen so little of you since your birth.

The legacy that Thompson left to future generations was indeed a many-faceted one. He helped to found the town of Hamilton, Missouri, and he provided leadership for the development and growth of St. Joseph, his adopted city. He designed bridges and built levees that were still in use years after his death. He wrote poetry and authored proclamations that helped to shape public opinion. He fathered six children, four of whom survived him, one son and three daughters. His son, Henry Bolivar, became well-known and respected across the state of Louisiana for his skill as state engineer and his active participation in the state militia. His daughters served in leadership roles in their communities, and Marcie has been described as a talented musician and writer. While he himself was in prison, Thompson made many humanitarian contributions to the families of other prisoners of war. Although denied the Confederate general's commission he yearned for, he played a unique role in the war and then set an example for peace and patriotism when the war was over.

About a month before his death, Thompson was interviewed by a reporter from the *St. Joseph Gazette,* who wrote of him:

> General Thompson is a fascinating man, apparently about fifty years of age, tall and slender as a boy of eighteen, with clean-shaven chin and closely-trimmed mustache, small keen eyes, large, positive mouth, broad forehead and massive lower jaw, together with a nervous, earnest manner while engaged in conversation—he impressed one as being a remarkable man. He is a fair type of the Southerner, physically; the Northerner, mentally, and the Westerner, in his manner and broad progressive ideas. He is a Virginian by birth and a cosmopolite in experience, ideas and manner.

A newspaper story announcing Thompson's death and burial closed by saying: "We may well exclaim, 'Here lies one whom everybody loved, who loved to benefit mankind, and whom, when his mission was accomplished, took his flight to a better and brighter world.' May heaven give us more such men as Jeff Thompson."

Epilogue

~

In the official history of the United States, Missouri is recorded as a state loyal to the Union during the Civil War, and many citizens accepted without question that Missouri in fact remained a part of the Union. However, many others, like Jeff Thompson, were sympathetic to the South, and when the Confederate Congress admitted the state to the Confederacy, it staked its own claim to Missouri's loyalty. A divided state was the result; a deadly guerrilla war wracked the state for four years, and when the war finally ended, Missouri citizens faced the daunting task of relearning how to live and work together.

Missouri made very large financial contributions to the war effort. Beyond the monetary value of its slaves, freed in early 1865, the state also suffered enormous financial losses: in 1868 its taxable wealth was $46 million less than it had been in 1860. Tax collections fell sharply during the war, and the state had to spend more than $7 million equipping and maintaining troops, although most of this was eventually repaid by the federal government.

Missouri also contributed its manpower, providing many military leaders for the North, including General Ulysses S. Grant and General Frank Blair, and even more for the South, including Confederate General Sterling Price, General John S. Marmaduke, and State Guard General M. Jeff Thompson. According to Edwin

C. McReynolds in his book *Missouri: A History of the Crossroads State,* more than fourteen thousand Missourians in the Union Army and four thousand Missouri Confederates died in combat, a fearsome toll indeed.

No major battles were fought in Missouri. In fact, Dwyer's *A Compendium of the War of the Rebellion* classifies only one as a legitimate battle—Wilson's Creek, regarded by many as the most famous of the state's Civil War engagements. The other clashes are listed as skirmishes, actions, or engagements. However, Missouri provided the sites for 1,162 engagements of the war, or 11 percent of the total for all the states—more than any other state except Virginia and Tennessee.

But the greatest toll taken by the long, bloody war was in terms of human anguish. As Preston Filbert writes in *The Half Not Told: The Civil War in a Frontier Town,* quoting from a young woman's diary, "Who can record the sorrow and destruction that has been brought to so many hearts or count the orphans and widows or measure the tears that have fell?"

Clearly, the Jeff Thompson family offers a prime example of the suffering brought about by the ravages of war. Like many another soldier, he was separated from his loved ones for the duration of the war. He died at the age of fifty of tuberculosis contracted in prison camp. His wife, Emma, found the burden of rearing four children alone and undergoing such frightening experiences as having her home vandalized and, when she fled to St. Louis, being arrested under suspicion of being a Confederate spy, overwhelming. She had several emotional breakdowns and had to be committed to an asylum.

At that time, mental institutions were called insane asylums or lunatic asylums. The Fulton State Hospital opened in 1851 as the State Lunatic Asylum. It and the State Insane Asylum at St. Louis, established in 1869, and the State Lunatic Asylum at St. Joseph, which opened in 1874, were fortress-like complexes where the patient-prisoners were shut away from the world and often subjected to such treatments as lobotomies, icy baths, and bleeding, and were sometimes locked in their rooms or chained to their beds. Because of the stigma surrounding mental illness, these patients were at best misunderstood and at worst neglected or even abandoned by their families, and in many instances, when they died, few traces of their having lived were left behind.

In the case of Thompson's wife, very little is known about her hospitalization or death. Although Jeff was buried in Mount Mora, the cemetery records provide no evidence that Emma was interred there, although some records are missing. It was not uncommon for patients of mental institutions to be buried on the asylum's premises. After the State Lunatic Asylum at St. Joseph closed as a mental institution, the burial grounds were sodded over and a single stone erected to represent the graves of all those who had been buried there.

Even the year of Emma's death is unclear—an unsigned hand-written document among the documents at Tulane University titled "The Family of General M. Jeff Thompson" states that she died in 1868 "soon after the war"—then that date is crossed out and the year 1884 is substituted.

When Jeff Thompson's lengthy obituary was published in the *St. Joseph Gazette,* it included very detailed information about his life and listed his survivors, but made no reference to his wife or whether she still lived. One frustrated researcher trying to locate information about Emma remarked that she "might as well not have existed."

In 1848, on her way west to California with her father, Emma Catherine Hayes could not have foreseen the events that lay ahead for her when she met and married M. Jeff Thompson. Like so many others, her life was to be devastated by the War Between the States.

For Further Reading

~

Across Five Aprils, by Irene Hunt (New York: Berkley Books, 1986), although a juvenile novel, is appropriate for readers of all ages. It presents a vividly realistic picture of the impact of the Civil War on families and individuals.

Battle Cry of Freedom: The Civil War Era, by James M. McPherson (New York: Ballantine Books, 1988), is a Pulitzer-prizewinning book that describes many facets of the war in a perceptive and very readable manner.

The Bootheel Swamp Struggle, by Marshall Dial (Lilburn, Missouri: Lloyd Publications, 1961), tells a fascinating story that includes many colorful incidents in Thompson's checkered career, especially those activities and movements that took place in southeastern Missouri and Arkansas.

The Civil War Experiences of General M. Jeff Thompson, by John Glendower Westover (unpublished master's thesis, University of Missouri, 1941), is a thoughtful, carefully documented analysis of Jeff Thompson's own account of his experiences in the first year of the Civil War. Westover's introduction provides useful biographical background.

The Civil War in Missouri as Seen from the Capital City, by Dino Brugioni (Jefferson City: Summers Publishing, 1987), focuses on a number of the colorful individuals who were major players in

Missouri during the Civil War, such as Claiborne Jackson, Sterling Price, John Fremont, and John Marmaduke.

The Civil War Reminiscences of General M. Jeff Thompson, edited by Donal Stanton, Goodwin F. Berquist, and Paul C. Bowers (Dayton: Morningside House, Inc., 1988), contains Jeff Thompson's memoirs and deals only with his war experiences. Thompson wrote vividly and sprinkled his writing with anecdotes, humor, opinions, and personal observations. Not a polished document, it nevertheless makes interesting reading and provides an insight into Thompson's character. In addition, the biographical discourse provided by the editors gives greater depth to the book.

The Half Not Told: The Civil War in a Frontier Town, by Preston Filbert (Mechanicsburg, Pennsylvania: Stackpole Books, 2001), paints a bleak picture of St. Joseph, Missouri, during the painful days of the Civil War—its divided loyalties and its depredation by Confederates, Federals, and guerrilla bands. Preston maintains that of all the young cities of the Midwest, St. Joseph was most brutally affected by the Civil War. Living in an occupied fortress, its citizens were disarmed and left helpless to defend themselves and unable to trust either their government or one another.

A History of Missouri, by E. M. Violette (St. Louis: State Publishing, Inc., 1954), is a very readable Missouri history and provides a context in which the events of the war took place, as well as other general information about the state.

Swamp Fox of the Confederacy: The Life and Military Services of M. Jeff Thompson, by James (Jay) Monaghan (Tuscaloosa, Alabama: Confederate Publishing Co., Inc., 1956), is a limited-edition book that tells Thompson's story in an entertaining and informative style. It includes information about Thompson before the war, with little emphasis on his postwar activities. Its primary focus is on Thompson's war years.

Voices of the Swamp Fox Brigade: Supplemental Letters, Orders and Documents of General M. Jeff Thompson's Command, 1861-1862, compiled and edited by James E. McGhee (Independence, Missouri: Blue and Grey Book Shoppe, 1999), is an invaluable resource for researchers wishing to trace Thompson's activities in southeast Missouri.

Primary sources that may be of additional interest to readers, such as Thompson's personal and military correspondence, his memoirs, photographs, and other pictures, newspaper and magazine clippings, and Thompson's poems—excerpts of which appear throughout this book—are not conveniently held in one location. The original handwritten memoirs, as well as typescripts, are among the Thompson papers in the Southern History Collection at the University of North Carolina. The University of Missouri Western Historical Manuscripts Collection in Columbia houses a typescript of the memoirs, newspaper and magazine articles, pictures of Thompson, and other items. The Missouri Historical Society in St. Louis holds important materials, and the Ohio Historical Society and the Scott County, Missouri, Historical Society also have materials relating to him. Especially fruitful to the serious researcher are the holdings in Special Collections, Howard Tilton Memorial Library, Tulane University, New Orleans. In addition, visitors to St. Joseph, Missouri, will find many reminders of Thompson, including murals and his grave site at Mount Mora Cemetery.

Index

Page numbers in italics refer to illustrations.

Index

Page numbers in italics refer to illustrations.

About the Author

Doris Land Mueller is the author of two books for children, *Small One's Adventure* and *Marryin' Sam*. She teaches at St. Louis Community College and lives in Fenton, Missouri.